"Every grocer, car dealer, car manufacturer, steel industrialist, software entrepreneur, restaurant owner, and hospital, resort, and airline CEO needs to read, take heed, and plead for change—if they don't want to hang out a 'going out of business' sign. Rulon Stacey's *Over Our Heads* isn't a fable; it's a serious reality check."

—D.A. Benton, Author, *CEO Material*

"Dr. Stacey's analogous account of the small town of Capital Springs promises to be the *Who Moved My Cheese?* of the healthcare industry. He is able to weave a compelling story that tells the history of the industry and provides insight into the foundation of our crisis. If you've ever wondered how we got to this point and whom we should blame, read *Over Our Heads*. It breaks a complex subject down to clear and concise terms that provide brilliant illumination and challenge our thinking on how we must approach the future."

—Britt Berrett, Phd, FACHE; President, Texas Health Presbyterian Hospital Dallas; Executive Vice President, Texas Health Resources

"In my career I've seen the healthcare industry from various sides: executive leadership, governance, and academia. I know the problems we face are complex and difficult. Still, I believe that with a clear understanding of how we ended up 'over our heads,' we can start to fight our way back to the surface. Dr. Stacey's book simplifies that history and shines a light on where we went wrong. His analogy is sure to resonate with healthcare professionals at every level."

—Errol L. Biggs, PhD, FACHE; Director, Graduate Programs in Health Administration; Director, Center for Health Administration; University of Colorado-Denver Business School

Over Our Heads

An Analogy on Healthcare, Good Intentions and Unforeseen Consequences

Rulon Stacey, PhD, FACHE

Published by:
Fire Starter Publishing
913 Gulf Breeze Parkway, Suite 6
Gulf Breeze, FL 32561
Phone: 850-934-1099
Fax: 850-934-1384
www.firestarterpublishing.com

ISBN: 978-0-9828503-1-2

Library of Congress Control Number: 2011923720

Printed in the United States of America

To my beautiful wife, Linda, and my four daughters,
Laura, Maria, Jennifer, and Catherine.
Thank you for your patience and guidance
as I have tried to run a grocery store.

TABLE OF CONTENTS

Foreword i

Acknowledgments iii

Introduction v

Chapter 1: A Grocer's Calling 1

Chapter 2: Seasons of Change 11

Chapter 3: To Feed a City 25

Chapter 4: The Price of Progress 33

Chapter 5: An Unfair Burden 45

Chapter 6: Enemy of the People? 61

Chapter 7: More Wrongs Don't Make a Right 81

Chapter 8: A City Forever Changed 99

Epilogue: Consequences 109

Appendix: United States Healthcare Timeline 125

Works Cited 131

Resources 133

About the Author 139

Foreword

Healthcare reform is a complex issue. I refer not only to the Patient Protection and Affordable Care Act that was signed into law in March of 2010, but to all the government programs that have been enacted over time and have gradually transformed our nation's healthcare system.

Here's what I like about *Over Our Heads*: It condenses this complicated, multi-layered history into a brilliantly simple analogy. It puts the current state of affairs into perspective for the reader, and does so in a memorable way.

I've found that people who are deeply knowledgeable on a particular subject are able to explain it to others in succinct and simple language. This is an ability I truly admire—and Rulon Stacey has mastered it.

Read this book and you'll come away with a clear and concise understanding—perhaps for the first time ever—of how our industry reached such a state of crisis in so (relatively) few years.

Like all good analogies, it's short and sweet. You may be able to read it in one sitting. (And it's such a great story you probably will!)

But here's my favorite aspect of the book. It shines a light on the compassionate, giving nature of healthcare professionals everywhere.

Just as the book's storekeeper, Andy Johnston, feels profoundly connected to his neighborhood and is proud to provide the food that sustains his customers, most healthcare providers have a powerful sense of responsibility for *their* communities and patients. It's in their DNA. I've worked with thousands of them throughout my career, so I know.

I truly believe there is no group of people as passionate, as committed, and as dedicated as those in healthcare. And no matter what solutions we may find for the challenges we face, it's these men and women who will make them work.

To them we at Studer Group offer our gratitude—and the hope that they'll always be able to provide the best possible care to the patients they serve.

Quint Studer

Acknowledgments

I would like to offer a special thanks to those groups and individuals who have allowed the idea of this book to become a reality. I extend my humblest gratitude:

To the employees, physicians, volunteers, board of directors, and most specifically the senior management team at Poudre Valley Health System. For more than a decade, you have shown me that a private, locally controlled health system can produce the best outcomes in the world. Each of you has been an inspiration to me.

To my mother and father, who taught me to work hard, smart, and honest at a young age, and to my three brothers and three sisters, all of whom have diligently loved and nurtured me all of my life.

To the various mentors and friends who have helped me throughout my entire career. I wish I could name each and every one but there are just too many of you.

To the best-selling author D.A. Benton for continuing guidance and encouragement from the very beginning.

To Charles Limley for editing this book for me. I am quite certain that you are the most gifted young writer in the country today. With your help, my thoughts took shape in a world you invented. Thank you!

And finally, I extend my utmost appreciation to Quint Studer and everyone at Studer Group who has played a part in bringing *Over Our Heads* to fruition. Thanks also to Bekki Kennedy and the team at De-Hart & Company Public Relations who worked hard to polish, proofread, and design my literary "baby." It goes without saying that without your help this book would never have happened.

Rulon Stacey

Introduction

For nearly two hundred years, Americans have searched for an effective, practical, and affordable means to access and provide healthcare. This search has been characterized by myriad ideas, solutions, and laws, many of which, I believe, have been proposed in an attempt to improve the state of the nation's healthcare system. However, these proposals and policies have instead created a system so convoluted and complex that simply keeping up with current policy has proven virtually impossible.

Over the past few decades, as the United States has continued seeking ways to make healthcare more accessible and affordable, the accompanying public debate has grown and increased in its intensity. Politicians on all sides have accused anybody, and very nearly everybody, as being the cause of our current healthcare crisis while failing to understand (or at least acknowledge) the true source of the problems.

Without this basic and fundamental grasp of cause and effect, we as a society have fallen into a pattern of passing law after law, all of which serve as bandages to cover over and staunch the bleeding of earlier policies, without ever stitching shut the wound.

In early 2010, this pattern continued as legislation designed to transform the entire American healthcare system was passed and signed into law. Because it fails to address the true root of the problems facing the system—and, indeed, exacerbates those problems—this act will, I believe, simply accelerate the train of American healthcare to breakneck speed as it continues its suicidal course toward the cliff's edge.

A significant cause of the current misunderstanding regarding the unreasonably high costs of healthcare revolves around public figures, politicians, and others who have, whether intentionally or not, created public spectacles that fuel fears far more than actually addressing concerns or explaining issues. Because such displays have become the dominant voices within the healthcare discourse, it has become extremely difficult to thoroughly and accurately address the real issues involved.

Often, the voices of healthcare providers and administrators are not only ignored, but demonized. Indeed, these individuals are popularly characterized as heartless machines whose greedy and inhumane actions have done more to create our problems than to provide quality patient care. Beyond my personal aversion to such characterizations, these types of depictions all too often silence a valuable and much-needed perspective on the state of the nation's healthcare system.

While there are many examples of ways in which the current healthcare situation has been inaccurately portrayed to the public, I will here outline four of the most notable vehicles:

Hollywood

In the 2002 film *John Q,* a distressed father holds a hospital emergency room hostage, demanding treatment for his son as ransom. The hospital's director, Rebecca Payne, plays a very convincing, yet in my experience entirely inaccurate, hospital executive. She not only refuses to address the father's plight, but also does nothing to help the overall situation, thereby demonstrating an undeniable contempt for the father, his family, and the healthcare industry in general.

Within the film, Rebecca Payne is an easily disliked character, and, sadly, it is this type of stereotypical portrayal that has come to embody the popular and inaccurate image of the healthcare situation in general, and healthcare executives specifically.

In direct contrast to this negative portrayal, my experience has been that the healthcare executive—much like the grocer of the story you are about to read—has spent his or her career working to improve the cost and quality of care for those who are being served.

Literature

In 2009, at the height of the national debate over healthcare reform, it came to my attention that there were many in the United States Senate who had been reading *The Healing of America: A Global Quest for Better, Cheaper, and Fairer Health Care* by T. R. Reid. Those leaders who had read the book then used much of its information in formulating their own opinions and, subsequently, in shaping the future of healthcare for the nation as a whole. The fact that senators drew such meaningful conclusions from this book is problematic, as it is often factually incorrect and works to perpetuate the myths commonly used to create public hysteria.

There are numerous inaccuracies within *The Healing of America*, but none are more telling than Reid's attempt to compare the U.S. healthcare system to others around the world by writing, "For the 45 million uninsured Americans, we're Cambodia, or Burkina Faso, or rural India" (287).

Not only is this statement factually inaccurate, it is irresponsible. To suggest that access to healthcare in the United States, even for the 10 to 15 million Americans who are uninsurable, is comparable to such regions of the world is a prime example of ways in which public spectacles are constructed with nothing more than outlandish claims and the intent to instill fear and panic in the American population. To think that national policy is being created and signed into law based on this type of information can be described only as frightening.

Politics

During the past decade, there has been ample evidence that policy-makers simply don't understand the impact that their actions will have on the overall healthcare industry.

For example, in December of 2003, President Bush signed into law the "Medicare Modernization Act" (MMA). This law was designed to help Medicare beneficiaries have access to increasingly expensive medications. However, it served only to expand the scope of Medicare without enhancing the process of paying for the services covered. Interestingly enough, this legislation provided subsidies to large employers while statutorily prohibiting the government from negotiating discounts with drug companies, or even establishing a formulary to create a list of approved drugs.

In 2009 the trend continued. Shortly after the election, President Obama spoke at multiple town hall meetings throughout the country in order to explain reform proposals and outline why he viewed such actions as both necessary and beneficial. During one such meeting, President Obama explained that healthcare reform is needed in order to ensure value for the product being purchased.

As an example, he pointed out that if an individual took his or her car to a garage to be repaired, and the car was then returned without being fixed, the customer would not be expected, nor should he or she feel responsible, to pay the garage. The implied argument of this analogy is that healthcare ought to be the same: If a patient goes to a doctor or hospital and is not made well, there should be no payment made for services provided.

Sadly, there is little in either the 2003 MMA or the auto repair analogy that accurately resembles either the design or the function of the American healthcare system. These two cases exemplify the type of political gesturing that creates public hysteria while illustrating the flawed reasoning and inaccurate language that have come to dominate political discussions around healthcare.

Most alarmingly, these examples clearly demonstrate that even those at the highest levels of our nation's government don't "get it." They don't get how our healthcare system works, and they don't get the underlying impact that public policy has had on creating the current healthcare crisis.

Research

In 2000, the World Health Organization (WHO) published a study ranking world healthcare systems. The United States was listed thirty-seventh overall, placing it well behind Colombia, Morocco, Chile, and others. More than any other source I have encountered, this list has been used (and is repeatedly referenced in Reid's book) to justify the need for healthcare reform in the United States. People, including those on Capitol Hill, continually reference this study in their depictions of U.S. healthcare as costing more and having worse outcomes than any other industrialized nation in the world.

By using this study or any reference to it, politicians imply that they know and understand the causes of our current healthcare crisis. In reality, focusing on sources such as the WHO study is like giving aspirin to a patient with an infection, masking the symptoms without solving the problems. The fact is that the WHO study was published in 2000 and reported on data collected in 1997. Even if its conclusions were accurate, to use this study as a major reference for public policy passed in 2010—fully thirteen years after the data was gathered—is simply bad science.

Furthermore, when one learns that the primary drivers for this study were political in nature and not clinical—for example, the study uses very ineffective and subjective measures such as "Overall Level of Health" and "Fairness of Financial Contribution" [see "World Health Organization Assesses the World's Health Systems"] in ranking the various healthcare systems of the world—the fact that the study is simply outdated becomes a secondary concern. The persistent use of this study is yet another indicator that the discourse surrounding American healthcare has become dominated by inaccurate, flawed, and heavily biased information.

These are just a few of the ways in which the nation's healthcare crisis is characterized and presented to the American people. Various forces ranging from political parties to producers of popular culture fail to address the fundamental issues involved. In the end, when the general public becomes influenced by such inaccurate data, the solutions that are then presented cannot, by definition, address the root of the problem. If America's healthcare dilemma is ever to be rectified, decision makers and voters *must* reach a correct understanding of its fundamental causes.

To this end, I have become interested in finding a way to better explain just what these causes are. Accordingly, I have developed the short story contained within the covers of this book. I hope it will serve as an effective analogy for outlining the primary reasons why the American healthcare system has reached the point it has today: expensive, complicated, and too often inaccessible. While I have attempted to identify the most crucial elements in the evolution (or perhaps degeneration) of our nation's healthcare system, I remain conscious of the fact that there are such a vast number of factors contributing to the problems facing us today that it is ultimately impossible to fully and accurately account for each and every one.

I would also like to add that my intent is not to point the finger of blame at any particular political figure or party for our current crisis. The two mayors who appear in this story, Ted Sprine and Stride Pen, are symbolic of the many leaders who have played a role in shaping American healthcare—although the latter figure, admittedly, will call to mind the creators of the recent public policy process. (Readers may note that both names are comprised of the letters that make up the word "president.")

With that said, I believe the following analogy, while admittedly not perfect, will relate the story of American healthcare in a way that is easily understandable. With this analogy, it is my hope that all people, regardless of prior healthcare knowledge, will more accurately and fully understand how our current system has reached its present predicament.

As the analogy proceeds, I have included references within each chapter to the historical and factual events being represented. In this way, readers may gain a broad perspective of the history of healthcare in the United States, as well as a better understanding of what various healthcare policies mean in practice and what their ultimate results are for us as a nation.

The concluding epilogue represents a projection into the future of American healthcare if we are unable to alter its current course. Finally, it is important to point out that as complicated as the healthcare system is portrayed as being in this book, I simply could not include all the complexities of the healthcare system in this analogy. In short, even though the situation depicted in this book is complex and frustrating, the reality is far *more* complex and frustrating.

In seeking solutions to our current healthcare problems, an accurate understanding of how these problems came about is critical. It is my hope that this brief and simple analogy will accomplish just that by illuminating the process through which America's healthcare crisis was born.

And now, welcome to Capital Springs, the city where you will begin to understand not only how complicated the healthcare crisis has become, but why....

Rulon F. Stacey, 2011

CHAPTER ONE

A Grocer's Calling

The Johnstons had become a part of Capital Springs. Their small storefront on the corner had become a natural element of the city's landscape, and everyone in the neighborhood knew them, or at least their name. In short, they were a fixture, a permanence, a literal piece of the city.

The Progress of "More"

Long ago, Capital Springs had been built around a large underwater spring from which clear water, after somehow managing to push and slip its way through the deep and tight places of the earth, finally bubbled up and over the rocky lip of a wide pool before quickly running down the hill to join the fast-moving river below.

In the early days of the settlement, this spring provided much-needed clean water, and consequently became a natural meeting place for the few families working to build their lives on the surrounding land. This first small group of settlers gradually grew into a few dozen families and eventually, as people began building houses nearer to one another and small shops appeared, the city of Capital Springs was born. (And, of course, the bubbling spring was its proud centerpiece.)

Despite its central importance to those first settlers, as well as its place in the city's very name, the spring was eventually buried under the clamor for more. People continued to move to this new and promising city, demanding as they did so more stores, more goods, more houses, more offices. Decades passed, and when the automobile finally became popular, the cry was for more pavement, more roads, more sidewalks, anything as long as it was *more*.

Layer after layer of smoothed-out dirt, poured concrete, expanding shops, grasping office buildings, and the sprawling apartments and suffocating tenements needed to house all those who were demanding "more" began to encroach on the wide and constant pool of the spring. As more and more people moved to the city to work in its growing factories and to buy from its hulking stores and thriving merchants, the city diverted the spring's water into various channels flowing in different directions in order to provide its rapidly expanding population with more and more water.

Under this strain, and over the seemingly endless years, the spring began to change. It shrank. The flowing course of its water was shifted to accommodate the flow of traffic until finally, beneath generations of "more" and layer upon layer of "more," the spring was covered over and its waters were again forced underground. It had been transformed into something no longer useful—it had morphed beyond recognition or rescue. Its water, once the lifeline of the settlement and for which the city was named, had been corked and forced back underground by the increasing demand for more.

The spring had lain dormant for so long that even Grandpa Johnston had missed it by several generations. By the time he arrived, Capital Springs was a large and busy city, and, bristling with skyscrapers, it had no room for pools, mud, streams, rivers, and certainly not the bubbling of springs.

A Market and a Mainstay

Upon arriving in the city, Grandpa Johnston had just enough money to begin renting a small building on the corner with one large glass window facing the road. Sleeping in the back room, he began selling groceries.

Three generations later, Johnston's Corner Market had become a regular fixture in the large and dense landscape of the city. The neighborhoods from Fifth Street down to Eighth Street shopped here, and between these regular customers and the various other people living or working in this section of the city, the Corner had remained busy through the course of its history.

"It was my grandfather who opened this place. He got it all started," recalled Andy Johnston. He had just finished sweeping the floor when his friend Karl wandered into the shop. After putting the broom away, Andy settled into his chair behind the front counter, and the men's conversation wandered aimlessly in and out of the past.

"Grandpa went through a lot to get this business going, and now I really feel like I have too," Andy reflected, his eyes sweeping the shelves in front of him. "But—and I feel pretty good about saying this now—I think we pulled through it all right, and all that stuff's over now. The whole time things were rough, the one thought that really bothered me was that the Corner might not survive for me to hand over to Stephen someday."

"Yeah, I can understand that," replied Karl Helgason, who lived around the corner on Sixth and Broadway, and who had grown up in the neighborhood with Andy. "Those were some pretty rough days, and it had to have been worse for you than maybe anybody else. I mean, everybody still had to eat and feed their kids, and most people just couldn't afford it." He paused and looked down at his hands before continuing. "I know you gave a lot yourself to make sure everyone had food, and it must have been tough. I think it's pretty much over, too, but I'm sure there are still some people who haven't quite bounced back."

"Yeah, you're definitely right," said Andy, standing up from his chair and running a thick hand through his dark hair. Andy was a man of average height with broad shoulders and a belly that had slowly and steadily worked its way outward over the years to create a slight overhang above his belt buckle. All of this seemed somehow to enhance the contented nature of his smile, which made regular appearances as he spoke.

"Everybody's got to eat, and that's what the Corner's for—it's what I'm here for," he stated as though this truth should have been self-evident. "Things were really tough for a while, but it seems like most people have jobs now, and it looks like for the most part things are back on track."

"Well, from everything I've heard, you really helped people survive and make it through, and you're a good man for doing what you did," Karl said appreciatively. "We always seem to figure things out somehow, and I know you really helped pull everyone through it this time." He leaned over and clapped his friend on the shoulder. "Anyway, I'd better get going and let you get back to work."

With that, Karl waved and left the store, holding the swinging glass door open for a young woman who smiled at his polite gesture.

After wandering the aisles for a few minutes, the woman who had just entered approached the register and, emptying her basket, placed a gallon of milk, a loaf of bread, a carton of eggs, a few boxes of cereal, and a small assortment of canned vegetables and fruit before Andy.

"Did you find everything all right?" he asked pleasantly, scanning her items.

"Yes, thank you."

"Your total will be seventeen fifty-three."

After paying, though, the woman remained at the register, looking down at her feet and clearly hesitant to take hold of her grocery bags.

"Is there anything else I can help you with?" asked Andy, a bit puzzled.

"No, well, yes, I mean…yes. Yes, that's everything I need," the woman stumbled, reaching across the counter to retrieve her groceries. Just before touching them, however, she dropped her hand limply back to her side and raised her eyes to Andy's, a determined set to her mouth.

"Yes, you're right, I do need some help." Her tone was still soft, but she didn't falter. "Do you have any discounted food? I mean, maybe any damaged or broken or expired stuff I can buy for cheap?" The questions now rushed from her mouth in a stream of agitated earnestness. "See, this just isn't enough for three kids," she said, tossing her hand toward her two small and crumpled bags of food. "But that's all I can really afford right now. I'll buy anything you can't sell regularly, if you can somehow give it to me for cheap."

Andy placed both hands on the counter before him and looked down at them, thinking. *How fitting*, he thought, *that this woman and these questions should come only minutes after the conversation with Karl.* Certainly things were better now, but clearly not everyone had recovered. *Even when things are good*, he thought, *people still struggle.*

Looking back up into her quiet, expectant eyes, Andy was flooded with a rush of memories and thoughts that carried him back through the trying times of recent years.

An Uphill Battle

Even today, nobody really understood what had caused everything to slide downhill. All anyone knew was that suddenly, years ago, factories began closing, offices stopped hiring and began shutting down altogether, people lost their jobs, and soon it seemed as if everyone was struggling just to take care of themselves and their families.

To make things worse, some of the city's banks had fallen apart and closed their doors, destroying with their crumbling establishments entire lifetimes' worth of working, saving, and dreaming. Many in

Capital Springs lost all they had. After that, so many other stores and small shops began closing that Andy had begun to worry about his own.[1]

---

① The Healthcare Connection: *The Ripples of Recovery*

The Great Depression of the 1930s helped establish a broad system of government-operated welfare programs, which in turn gave rise to new conceptualizations of the government's role within the realm of medicine. In short, a system of government-sponsored healthcare, which, "when first proposed, seemed to some reformers as 'outrageously radical,' by 1933 had become part of a 'new concordance' about what should be done to revitalize the Nation" (Corning).

The economic problems of Capital Springs eventually became so widespread that many people were unable to afford food, and so Andy had worked with them, providing discounts or giving food to people entirely on credit with no interest or payment due dates. He had always remained focused on doing whatever was needed to ensure that his neighborhood and his customers ate. During this time, he began to be haunted by the thought that he, the third generation to own Johnston's Corner Market, might become the last.

The realization that a failure to keep the Corner alive would translate directly into a failure to have anything to pass along to his own son weighed heavily on his mind; but now, after trudging through many months of decreasing financial accounts and shrinking bank balances, it seemed as if everything had recovered. From what he could see, many of his neighbors had been able to find new jobs, and it seemed as if Capital Springs had managed to pull itself out of the worst economic slump of its history. Every day, the radio, television, and newspapers were filled with reports of new businesses and factories opening and of new growth for the city. Andy felt that the Corner had survived its hardest times yet, and he was proud that he and his neighborhood had come out on top.

But still, there was this woman. Andy's thoughts came rushing back to the present, and he looked up from where his hands still lay on the counter. *People still struggle*, he repeated in his mind, *and it's up to us to help each other out of it.*

More Than "Just Business"

"Things are still a little tough, huh? Well, I'm sure they'll get better," Andy told his customer with a reassuring smile. "Let's see what we can find."

Motioning for the woman to follow him, he opened the old wooden door leading to the back room where Grandpa Johnston had once slept. Despite its modest size, this room now served as the Corner's storeroom as well as Andy's office. In one corner sat a desk with a lamp, a chair, and a filing cabinet, while the rest of the room was filled almost to bursting with boxes, bags, and shelves of food.

"We usually keep any damaged goods here and try to have them returned to our distributor for new stuff," Andy explained as he and the woman entered the room. "There's nothing wrong with the actual food itself, though, so if we can't return anything for some reason, we usually donate it all to the shelter."

Chuckling to himself and picking up a can with a wedge-shaped dent in its center, he continued, "I always wonder how some of this stuff gets so beat up. I guess it's a rough life though, you know. I mean, look at this soup. Somebody makes a giant batch of the stuff, puts it in a can for somebody else to eat…but before it ever gets to its destination, it trades hands so many times."

Out of the corner of his eye, Andy noticed that the woman's rather nervous expression was beginning to relax into a tentative smile, so he continued his monologue.

"Think about it. This can has been stacked on pallets, carried by forklifts, carted around warehouses, loaded and shipped on trucks, and finally stacked up here on my shelves. It probably couldn't help getting a few dents and tears along the way. Really, it's a wonder this stuff arrives here still edible at all, and not smashed to bits in some warehouse somewhere."

The woman nodded, reaching up to hook a wayward strand of hair behind her ear.

"Ah, here we go," said Andy, setting the can down and pulling a large cardboard box, ragged and torn at the corners, out into the center of the room. "Looks like this is everything I've got right now."

Inside the box was an assortment of canned vegetables, soups, stews, and sauces. All of them had large dents in the sides and a few were missing labels altogether, making their contents entirely unknown. There were also a few boxes of cornbread mix, torn open and spilling their contents onto the bottom of the tattered box.

"Is it possible for me to buy some of this?" asked the woman, looking down hopefully at the disorderly pile. "I mean, I know you're trying to return them, but I could pay something for them, too. I don't mean to be a nuisance or a bother or anything, but if there's any way you could sell me some of this…"

"Well, I'd rather you had it than sending it all back anyway," Andy stated, interrupting her. "Yeah, take as much as you need. Anything here that you can get back home—consider it yours. And don't worry about the money either."

Clearly taken aback, she blinked a few times before answering in a voice that trembled slightly, "I don't know how to thank you for this. I feel so bad even asking, but I just don't know what else to do. I mean, after I lost my job—and me alone with the kids—it's all been so hard, and I just don't know what to do anymore. Thank you so much. Thank you."

"I know, believe me, I know," Andy responded with a faint smile. "I've got a son of my own at home. I understand."

After loading the worn cans of food into bags and helping the young woman to the door, Andy returned to his seat behind the counter. Glancing toward the back room of the shop, he thought of his grandfather, sleeping on the floor of that room, and of his own father, who first showed him the joy of being a grocer. It struck Andy that just as there had always been some way for them to work through whatever problems they had faced, he could do the same.

He thought about the woman, now walking toward her home and her children, and knew that this was why he loved the Corner. It was not just selling food or trying to make money that interested him. The Corner wasn't simply a business. It was part of the community. He had known many of the people who came to the shop for years, and he had helped most of them when jobs were lost and living became difficult. He was glad for these opportunities to help—this was what it meant to be a grocer.

That evening, after turning out the lights and locking the Corner's door behind him, Andy walked the three blocks to his brownstone apartment building. Looking up at the trees that lined the streets, he watched their fading yellow and brown leaves fall haphazardly in lazy spirals to the sidewalk below. Maybe these trees were old enough to remember the first bubbling water. How many winters had they watched before opening up again in the spring?

Life is always changing, thought Andy. He had already seen so much in Capital Springs change. He had watched the city fall and build itself up again, and he wondered now what new changes he would encounter in the future.

CHAPTER TWO

Seasons of Change

As the weeks passed, Andy watched the trees that lined the city streets shed more, and finally all, of their leaves. He was glad, though, that as nature prepared for winter most other aspects of life around the Corner stayed the same. He had been worried about the possible effects of colder weather on some of the neighborhood's inhabitants, but so far nothing untoward had happened. And he hadn't seen the young woman who had asked for discounted food again. He hoped that was a good thing.

A Safety Cushion

"Hey, did you catch old Sprine's speech last night?" Karl asked one winter morning. It was Saturday, and Andy had only just unlocked the Corner's door and taken off his coat in preparation of beginning work for the day.

"Oh, hey. No, I didn't. Anything new?"

Karl raised his eyebrows. "You haven't seen the paper either?"

Andy shook his head. "Not yet. I just got here and haven't even had time to really open the shop, let alone read anything," he chuckled, walking behind the counter and facing his friend. "You always run in here too quick—I can't get anything done!"

Karl rolled his eyes, acknowledging the joke as he slapped the paper onto the counter and pointed at a specific block of text. "Well, here it is. Take a look at this article."

CAPITAL SPRINGS—In a press conference yesterday, Mayor Ted Sprine proposed a new bill, which he hopes will become the cornerstone of financial security for Capital Springs, while also addressing any concerns still lingering in the wake of the city's past economic recession.

"This program will work to ensure the safety and security of all citizens so that any future economic slumps will not have the same negative effects," the mayor said. "Under this plan, all citizens of Capital Springs will be able to build a financial safety cushion for themselves and their families."

Sprine's program, dubbed the Citywide Safety Bill, or CSB, will increase income taxes by 6 percent. The additional tax revenue will then be added to the CSB Fund where it will be re-distributed to contributors at the time of retirement or other extreme instances of unemployment or disability.[2]

"A slight increase in taxes will allow for a foundation of funding, which will then be given back as monthly installments, essentially creating a citywide retirement plan," Sprine said. "This is its design, but the CSB also simultaneously creates a safety net if other issues make earning an income no longer feasible."

Sprine has recently come under fire from opponents who view this latest announcement as nothing more than a well-timed political move as the city prepares for the beginning of another election year.

Following yesterday's announcement, Sprine expressed his hope to pass the CSB into law during the coming months, and despite some criticism, an early survey shows that approval ratings are up from last winter, suggesting a potentially strong start for Sprine's campaign team as they begin planning for next year's election.

② The Healthcare Connection: *Security for All*

The Social Security Act was passed August 14, 1935. Although it did not initially include health insurance, its aim was to help create "a structure of permanent social welfare institutions. Since then, a broad and continuing role in social welfare matters has become accepted as part of the responsibility of the Federal Government" (Corning). Following the passage of this act, and in keeping with the new precedent established by it, government-funded healthcare became a legitimate topic of discussion and debate.

"Huh," Andy said under his breath, handing the paper back to Karl.

"So, what do you think?" his friend asked.

Andy sat back on his stool and stroked his chin. "I guess it sounds fine to me," he ventured. "We don't know much about it right now, but so far I guess it sounds all right."

"Yeah, we'll see how it all plays out. I wonder about all that stuff at the end of the article though. Elections are always interesting, and I wonder what will happen when all the campaigns really get going," Karl replied, rolling the newspaper back up and stuffing it into the front pocket of his jacket, apparently signaling the end of that discussion. "Hey, how's the kid these days? Haven't seen Stephen around for a while."

"Oh, he's fine," Andy answered, walking back around the counter to stand beside his friend. "Stephen's busy with school and everything else, but he's doing really well. I think he might have some time to start coming back in here once in a while when the semester lightens up a bit."

Happiness, Heartbreak, and Back Again

As usual, even the most oblique reminder of Andy's marriage caused his thoughts to spiral back into the past. He had met his wife, Jessica, twenty-three years ago at a party while celebrating his and some friends' graduation from college. After that first night, they dated throughout the following summer and were married eleven short months later.

Andy felt that the early years of his marriage were in many ways the highlight of his life, for while he and Jessica did not lead what most would consider a glamorous existence, nor had they by any means grown wealthy, they had been consistently and simply happy. After six years of marriage, Andy took over the Corner from his father, and he and Jessica began operating the store together. Later that same year, Jessica gave birth to their only child, Stephen, and the three of them lived their lives contentedly for two more years before tragedy found them.

Shortly after celebrating their eighth wedding anniversary, Jessica became seriously ill. Despite Andy's prayers that her ailment would prove to be curable, it was discovered that breast cancer had spread throughout much of her body. By this point the disease had grown too severe to be touched by medicine, and after three agonizing months, Jessica Johnston passed away.

Andy had never felt more crushed by anything in his entire life. He removed himself from the Corner and spent most of his days in the apartment with his two-year-old son. In this self-imposed exile, it had been Stephen who ultimately provided Andy with the sense of meaning and purpose that he needed to pick up the pieces of his life.

As the first deep bruises of loss slowly began to heal, Andy started the process of returning to life. He came back to the Corner and very gradually rediscovered his old sense of happy contentment, despite the thick and jagged scar left behind on his soul. Since the heavy trials of those days, Andy had always been grateful for Stephen and the way in which he had called him back, given him meaning, and reminded him of the beautiful parts of living.

Stephen, now sixteen years old, attended Capital Springs High School, and like Andy, seemed happy with his small corner of the world. He usually helped around the shop during the summers away from class, and during the school year would stop by whenever he had free time away from friends, homework, and studying. Andy noticed that this year, however, his son's visits were increasingly scarce. He was fairly confident this absence had something to do with a certain "just a friend" from school named Maria—and he had to admit to himself that he really didn't mind as long as his son was content.

Overall, Andy took his role as a parent seriously and continually wondered what impressions he might be making on his son. Through-out his years as a father, he had tried to be living proof that the world is an immensely large place, and that even neighborhood grocers can carry out a meaningful existence within it. He always felt that Stephen's short sixteen years of life had been happy and successful ones, and he hoped that somehow his efforts had contributed to that fulfillment, even if only in some small way. Andy knew that his son, regardless of anything he himself had done, was already somebody to look up to, and saw in him an individual who possessed the natural ability to find enjoyment in life regardless of position, role, or title.

So far, Stephen seemed to enjoy helping out at the Corner, and Andy hoped that when the time came, his son would choose to take over the family business, just as he had. Whether or not this ever actually happened, though, Andy remained determined to follow the examples of his father and grandfather and to keep Johnston's Corner Market in good enough condition to be able to offer it to Stephen whenever that day did come. It was his goal simply to have something worthy to give his son.

"Well, it'll be good to see him again," Karl said, bringing Andy back to reality. "He's always been a good kid. You'll have to tell him I say hello." He dug into the other pocket of his jacket, pulled out a green knitted stocking cap, and pulled it down onto his head.

"I'm headed off. Take it easy, Andy," he finished as he pushed open the front door and stepped outside, where his breath immediately turned to steam in the cold air of the morning.

"All right, see you later, Karl," Andy called.

Like Father, Like Son

As the winter deepened, the new year began. The cold months continued to march by, and Andy's walks between home and the shop eventually became soggy as the snow covering the roads turned to brown slush that was splashed up onto the sidewalk by the constant hustle of cars and buses. The sun awoke earlier in the morning and accompanied him later in the evening on his walks, and soon the leaves that had been shaken from their limbs by the winds of fall and covered over by the snows of winter began to free themselves from the melting ice. They created a damp carpet smelling of wet mold and the growth of new things.

That spring, Karl began visiting the Corner more often, always anxious to discuss the growing excitement and debates of the election year. Karl brought the newspaper, Andy turned on the radio behind the front counter, and they would discuss the latest speeches, debates, and news regarding the race between Mayor Ted Sprine, who was running for re-election, and his primary competitor, Reid Pents.

In this way, the months sped through the city, soon carrying with them the long days of summer. The school year finally ended, and Stephen once again returned to help his father at the Corner, glad to have another year of classes behind him and the relative freedom of summer ahead.

Early each morning, Andy and Stephen walked the three blocks from their apartment to the grocery store, enjoying the stillness of the city as the sun tossed down its first beams of warm yellow light. Leaving the apartment this early, they were some of the very few people on the sidewalks, and even the occasional car that passed seemed to respectfully defer to the hush of the morning. The rare silence gave them the impression that the slightly damp morning air, the pale young light of the sun, and even the tall city itself were somehow created and continued to live just for them.

In these moments, Andy fell in love with his life all over again. He thought of Jessica; he looked at his son. He considered their small brown apartment, the Corner, Capital Springs—everything seemed somehow to fit together, and he smiled.

"This is great," Andy pronounced on one such morning, shortly after opening the store for the day. Now that it was warm, he would often prop the front door open with a phone book to better enjoy the weather. On these days the noises of the city—cars, buses, road and building construction, bicycle bells, voices, scraps of conversation or music—somehow melted into a single and lively melody.

"I think we're selling more now than we have for years, and with both of us here, we can get twice as much done, and in half the time."

"Yeah, it's definitely a good summer so far," Stephen replied, emerging from the back room with a box of oranges. He had already grown taller than his father, and like Jessica, had a thin vertical build with light freckles and brown hair.

"I guess now, with no classes and homework to save me, you really get to put me to work, huh?" he added, grinning from above the box he was carrying. "Speaking of which, do you want me to get to the canned food after I finish the produce?"

"No, if you do the produce now, I'll get going on that other stuff, unless a customer comes in. Thanks," said Andy, turning on the radio's morning news before entering the back storeroom.

Just as Stephen had cut open the box and was beginning to arrange the oranges, an old man with short white hair whom neither Andy nor Stephen had ever seen before entered the store.

"Good morning," he said, giving Stephen a nod as he worked his way slowly through the open doorway.

"Hi, how's it going? Need help finding anything?"

"Thanks, I'll be all right," the old man answered.

"Okay, well, I'll be right here if you do," Stephen told him. "Just let me know."

After watching the new customer disappear down an aisle, Stephen returned to stacking oranges, emptying his box before returning to the storeroom and carrying out fresh bags of apples and potatoes. By the time he finished unloading these, the man was at the counter paying for his groceries, which Andy had put into bags.

"Thank you very much. Here's your change," Andy said to the man, handing back some bills and coins. "Need a hand getting everything out of here?" he asked, pointing at the brown paper bags.

"Oh, thank you, but I think I can manage. Have a good day," the man answered before laboriously gathering his purchases into his arms and making his way out the open front door.

After the customer had emerged onto the street and Andy was sure he was out of earshot, he called Stephen over to the counter. "Will you run out there real quick and see if that guy's really getting everything all right?"

"Yeah, sure," Stephen replied, setting down the bags he was working on and quickly striding through the doorway and around the corner. Turning onto Sixth Street, Stephen saw the old man nearly thirty yards ahead of him, shuffling slowly down the sidewalk, obviously struggling to do so while clutching one bag under each arm.

Jogging up behind the man, Stephen caught his attention, and, motioning toward the bag in the man's left arm, said, "Here, let me take this one for you. Where are we headed with these?"

"Oh yes, well…okay," replied the man, his initial surprise giving way to a thankful grin that wrinkled his thin face. "Well, yes, that's actually quite nice. I just need to get to the bus stop on the corner of Pike. Thank you," he finished, handing the bag over to Stephen.

"Well, if you've still got to get these groceries onto the bus and then somewhere else from there, I might as well give you a break and take them both," Stephen responded with a smile.

For the remainder of the short walk to the bus stop, the man told Stephen about growing up in Capital Springs. He found particular joy in pointing out which buildings had stood during his childhood and relating what each had once been used for and who had once owned them. Upon reaching the stop, Stephen waited with the man for the bus's arrival, after which he carried the bags on board, setting them down on the seat next to the old man. Apparently, the man now lived on the opposite end of the city, but said that he liked to visit other areas of Capital Springs once in a while, just to remember.

"Next time I'm around this neighborhood, I'll stop by," he said as Stephen left the bus to return to the Corner. "Thanks for everything."

One-Upping for Good

As summer continued wandering in and out of the Corner's open front door, Andy and Stephen fell into an easy rhythm of working together. These days, the upcoming elections were a constant source of interest, and anytime Karl came by the store, the topic quickly took over the majority of their conversations. The radio behind the counter was almost constantly on, alternating between music and the voices of people discussing the race for the mayor's office. Most recently, the voices on the radio had reported the success of Mayor Sprine's City-wide Safety Bill, which was enthusiastically passed into law midway through the summer.

This is Emily Clout, from station KVTU, bringing you all the latest election year updates, the radio sounded one morning as Andy and Stephen began the day's work of opening shop.

Not surprisingly, the economy has been a hot topic for this year's campaigns, Emily's voice continued, punctuated by a crackle of static every now and then. *Riding the hugely successful and popular Citywide Safety Bill, Mayor Ted Sprine holds a strong position in early pre-election surveys, with 68 percent reporting continued support of the incumbent nominee. Maintaining his position as the main competitor for the mayor's office and working not to be outdone, Reid Pents has begun introducing his own versions of economic welfare plans, many of which propose to build upon the CSB to provide increased public benefits and programs.*

"The race has really started now," Andy said knowingly to Stephen. "Every time one of them makes something happen, everyone else who wants the office has to promise the same thing, but they have to do the guy before them one better. Step everything up, you know. Sprine starts with the CSB, that's fine, but now Pents has to beat him out and offer something better. It's all a big race—a game to make everybody happy and get their votes."

As if to emphasize Andy's point, the radio continued: *Key among Pents's proposals is his focus on increasing government-sponsored payments to the sick, injured, and unemployed. Pents says that where the CSB focuses on providing security for the employed and retired, his plan will more effectively take into account the welfare of the truly needy. Most controversial of all, however, in his last public address, Pents sparked a new debate regarding food distribution within the city. Calling food the most basic of human necessities, Pents proposed working to build a system of government-funded food distribution for those in need. Citing the first ever Citywide Wellness Survey, conducted in the wake of the city's most devastating economic downturn, Pents concludes that Capital Springs has a larger population of individuals unable to afford food than any other city in the state.*[2]

③ The Healthcare Connection: *Lagging Behind*

During the years 1935-1936, the federal government completed its first National Health Survey, which concluded that the United States had higher mortality from accidents *and* infant mortality rates than any other industrialized country. The survey also reported that a large portion of the nation's population was unable to afford the cost of medical care.

Throughout the last remaining weeks of summer, the radio continued to be heard at the Corner. By this time, talk of the fast-approaching election was on the lips of most people in Capital Springs, and Karl had plenty of ears willing to listen when he brought up the latest twist in the race.

Change for Capital City

Indeed, the campaigns of both Ted Sprine and Reid Pents had become a heated contest. The passage of the Citywide Safety Bill, while making Mayor Sprine more popular than ever, had also seemed to spark new ideas in the minds of many regarding the city's government and its purpose in their lives. Pents responded to the popularity of the CSB by continuing to speak about building new programs that would provide more financial benefits for more people than originally planned. Ultimately, it was the newly introduced food debate that became the most important issue during the months and weeks leading up to election day.[4]

④ The Healthcare Connection: *A Climate of Support*

As healthcare continued to become a major topic of debate throughout the mid- to late-1930s, politicians favoring the creation of a government-sponsored system of healthcare began focusing efforts on creating a "climate of support" for future action (Corning).

For many in Capital Springs, the CSB provided a new sense of security and protection, and although the mayor's office and the city government had never provided the city's people with food before, once the idea was suggested, it seemed to make sense. After all, such a program represented more security and more safety. It promised to support a larger portion of the city's population, and so, after the idea floated through radio waves and between the speaking tongues of the city's people, the concept of a government-funded food distribution program took firm shape in Capital Springs.

This new version of security and protection became a necessity in the minds of the city's people. Accordingly, they demanded it from their leaders, making it clear that votes would go only to the person who would provide exactly what they wanted.

The mayoral candidates, in turn, weren't stupid, and understanding this new connection between promising security and winning votes, both candidates continued the debate on how to provide food for the city. In the end, as the summer began melting itself away to make room for the soft-footed coming of fall, it was Ted Sprine who narrowly won the election and a new term as mayor of Capital Springs.

Wishing you a good morning, this is Emily Clout on station KVTU, the radio behind Andy's counter crackled the day after the votes were cast. *After the closest mayoral race in decades, many analysts feel that ultimately it was the passage of the Citywide Safety Bill that gave Ted Sprine the momentum needed to finally clinch this tight contest with Reid Pents. In his victory speech last night, Mayor Sprine spoke on the improving state of the economy, the CSB, and the future of Capital Springs. Here's a highlight of what was said:*

"Capital Springs, I thank you for your votes," the newly re-elected mayor's voice told listeners. *"We as a city are improving all the time, and we will continue to do so. With the passage of the Citywide Safety Bill, we have begun to build for ourselves and our city a strong safety net, and in the coming months and years, we will continue to add to this system of security.*

"As your mayor, I have formulated and will focus on addressing what I refer to as the Economic Rights of Citizens.[5] *Central among these is the right of each person in Capital Springs to pursue a healthy and happy life. With this as our focal point, I will work to ensure the protection of the city and each of its members. The keystone to the Economic Rights of Citizens is providing the necessities of life for our people, and so with this in mind, I promise to work toward creating a system of increased food distribution,*

ensuring that all within Capital Springs will be provided a basic supply of food."

---

⑤ The Healthcare Connection: *A Presidential Promise*

During his 1944 election campaign, President Franklin D. Roosevelt called for an "Economic Bill of Rights," and included in it the "right to adequate medical care" (Corning).

As Andy switched off the radio and began preparing for the work-day, he couldn't help but feel proud of his town. It was good to live among people who truly cared about the well-being of their fellow citizens, and it was even better to know that Capital Springs's leader was listening to what his constituents wanted for their community. Surely, a bright future lay ahead for everyone—and Andy was excited to see what part he, as a grocer, would play in building it.

CHAPTER THREE

To Feed a City

Following the debates, speeches, and discussions surrounding the city's election race, a particularly strong desire for a new program of food distribution had been created. Acting on this, and in combination with the apparent success of the Citywide Safety Bill, it didn't take Mayor Ted Sprine long to begin putting his promises into action.

A Nourishing Initiative

After narrowly defeating Reid Pents in the fall, Mayor Ted Sprine was officially inaugurated for another term as mayor at the beginning of the new year. Within weeks, he had proposed expanding the Citywide Safety Bill to include a system of providing free or inexpensive food to certain CSB beneficiaries. Although there were some throughout Capital Springs who remained skeptical and unsure of these new ideas, the momentum of Sprine's re-election proved strong enough to win favorable votes for the proposal from nearly all city officials.

By the time the mayor's new program of food distribution, now called Nourishaid,[6] was officially passed into law, all grocers within

Capital Springs—Johnston's Corner Market included—had learned how the program would work as well as how they were to perform their roles as food providers within it. Retired individuals who were receiving monthly payments from the CSB Fund now also began receiving a certain number of "food vouchers" as part of their payments. With these vouchers, they could shop at any grocery store that had chosen to participate in Nourishaid. The grocer would then be responsible for filing all vouchers with the city government in order to receive payment for anything sold to these customers.

⑥ The Healthcare Connection: *Accessible Healthcare Expands*

The Social Security Amendments of 1965 authorized the Medicare and Medicaid programs to provide various forms of health insurance to qualifying individuals.

Nourishaid was something entirely unknown and untried. It represented new possibilities for Andy, the Corner, and the entire city, and so Andy was willing to try it—at least long enough to see what its impact might be on his customers and on the shop.

In the middle of another busy school year, Stephen was unable to help his father, and so Andy made his walks to and from the Corner by himself. More importantly, however, he was forced to begin the Nourishaid program on his own and without the help of his son. Andy wouldn't have changed the fact that his son was getting a good education for the world, but he did wish that Stephen was able to witness firsthand what might be the beginning of a new era for the Corner and for Capital Springs.

The transition to the new system didn't take long. Soon, Andy began seeing customers use food vouchers as payment for the first time, and in just a few short weeks, it had become a regular and routine aspect of selling groceries at the Corner.

Vouchers in Action

"So how is this Nourishaid thing working out for you so far?" Karl asked one Saturday morning while flipping through the newspaper and leaning against the front counter. It was only ten in the morning, and already there were a number of people wandering the aisles of food.

"It's actually been really great," Andy answered without hesitation.

"Yeah?" Karl looked up from the paper. "Good."

"Yeah, I mean, I'm seeing a lot of brand new faces coming in here with those vouchers, and I'm just seeing more people in general," Andy went on, gesturing toward the already-busy aisles. "As far as I can tell, everyone with vouchers really is able to get whatever they need—and really good stuff, too. So overall, I think it's working out great."

Their conversation was momentarily interrupted as an older couple approached Andy's front counter, pushing a cartful of groceries.

"Hello. Did you find everything all right?" Andy asked them.

"Yes, we did, thank you," the man responded as his wife began placing their selections on the counter.

Andy started the process of ringing up the prices of the groceries and loading them into bags. "Uh-oh," the woman said abruptly, turning to her husband. "We forgot to get the meat for dinner tomorrow night. I'd better run back there quickly and find some."

Overhearing their conversation, Andy made a dismissive gesture. "Oh, here, I can go grab some for you. Don't want to make you walk clear to the back of the store just for one little thing," he said, making his way around the counter.

"Well, thank you very much; that's very kind," the woman answered. "We're paying with these Nourishaid vouchers, so is there anything in particular we can or cannot have?"

Andy shook his head. "Not really. You can get pretty much whatever you want. Do you want me to get you a steak?"

"Actually, that would be nice. We rarely buy anything like that, but if you're sure it's okay to get some steak with these vouchers, then that would be really great," the man answered, joining in the conversation. "Our son and his kids are coming over tomorrow for dinner, and this will be so helpful."

"Okay, I'll be right back," Andy said over his shoulder as he headed toward the back of the store.

Bending over the cooler, Andy rummaged through its contents, searching for a steak large enough to feed an extended family, and, in the end, decided it would be best to simply give his customers two steaks instead of only one.

"Oh my, I don't think we can really take both of these," the woman ventured, surprised, when Andy placed the two largest steaks he was able to find into a bag. "I mean, that would be great, and they look delicious, but can we really have that much food with only these vouchers to pay for it all?" She looked up at Andy, her brows drawn together.

"Everything's fine," he reassured her with a smile. "I just hope you have a fun dinner tomorrow with your family!" With that, he helped the couple out the door and resumed his place behind the counter.

"That's actually kind of amazing," Karl remarked, continuing their previous conversation, now more curious than ever for having witnessed Nourishaid at work. "So people can really get any type of food they want?"

"Yeah, pretty much," Andy confirmed. "Actually, most of the people on Nourishaid are starting to shop more often than they used to. A lot of folks come here needing more than they did in the past, and now with Nourishaid, they don't have to pick and choose what to get or not to get.[①] And that's great by me," he added, placing the couple's vouchers in an envelope in the top drawer of the cash register. "There are a lot of people around here who really need this kind of benefit, and I understand why the city wants to help them out."

⑦ The Healthcare Connection: *Unexpected Escalation*

Soon after the passage of Medicare and Medicaid, healthcare proved to be an elastic service, as patients utilized their new benefits more frequently than initially expected. Subsequently, the cost of operating these programs quickly began showing signs of rapid and uncontrollable escalation.

"And you get fully paid back for all that stuff?" Karl looked incredulous.

"Yeah, there's just some new paperwork I have to do to file all the vouchers with the city, but it works fine. Really!" Andy chuckled at his friend's still-skeptical expression.

"Plus, what's really nice is that they pay me back for all of my costs plus 2 percent more," Andy added, smiling, as he closed the register. "It works out great because now I can really focus on just making sure that everybody gets the best food I can possibly give them, and that they all get as much of it as they need. So yeah, it's definitely good for everybody—as long as the government can really afford it all, of course."[8]

⑧ The Healthcare Connection: *An Incentive for Increase*

In the early days of Medicare and Medicaid, healthcare providers were reimbursed for their services on a cost plus 2 percent basis. This ultimately "amounted to an open-ended proposition by offering hospitals a small bonus for each and every cost increase" (Mayes 27). By the early 1970s, the government's Medicare expenditures were doubling every five years, and the overall cost of healthcare skyrocketed so much so that "while the CPI increased 89 percent between 1966 and 1976, hospital costs grew a staggering 345 percent" (Mayes 27). Medicare and Medicaid thus clearly demonstrated their massive growth and cost potential.

"Wow, that's great. I'm glad it's working out so well," Karl replied, his eyebrows raised in surprise.

"If this keeps going the way it is, I'll be selling more groceries than ever before, and it already seems like there are more people than I've ever seen getting food whenever they need it," said Andy. He let his gaze wander over the increasingly crowded store. New shoppers were coming through the door at regular intervals. "I may actually have to hire some part-time help, or see if Stephen can somehow come in after school, or something. I've just been so busy it's almost too much for me alone," he mused.

Only the Best

It seemed that people all over Capital Springs shared the same excitement Andy felt. Nourishaid was beginning to foster the sense that more of the city's people were being cared for, protected, and, as a result, living well. For Andy, this was particularly important, because when he closed up the store each day, he felt that he'd truly fulfilled what he thought of as the ultimate purpose of a grocer: He was feeding his community.

Shortly after the passage of Nourishaid, Mayor Ted Sprine announced that the program was functioning well, but that it needed to be expanded beyond the current CSB enrollees so that more people might receive its crucial benefits. Because of the program's initial success, the city council quickly supported the mayor's planned expansion. Food vouchers were now given to individuals and families not receiving CSB benefits, but whose lack of income made it a struggle to afford the cost of food. This expanded version of Nourishaid debuted to great excitement as it served to solidify the growing feeling that everyone in the city would truly be taken care of.[9]

⑨ The Healthcare Connection: *More Beneficiaries on Board*

Within the context of the analogy, the extension of Nourishaid to more beneficiaries specifically represents the Medicaid portion of the 1965 Social Security Amendments.

With an even larger number of people able to receive vouchers, the Corner continued to welcome more new customers. The usual neighbors still continued to shop, of course, but new faces from other parts of Capital Springs were consistently swinging through the Corner's glass door, moving happily up and down its aisles, and filling grocery carts. With the expansion of Nourishaid, a rapidly growing number of Capital Springs's residents could now afford the food they needed, if not through wages earned at jobs, then through the aid of the city's increasingly popular government.

Andy's happiness grew as he was able to provide groceries to a larger portion of the city he loved. Because of the Nourishaid program, the Corner was now selling more groceries and growing faster than it had during any other point in its three-generation lifetime.

For the first time, Andy was able to order shipments of specialty produce, meat, and bread for all his customers, and he enjoyed watching this new assortment of high-quality food leave his shop in the arms of so many people. If somebody wanted apples, Andy sold them fruit from the finest harvest of the largest organic farms he could find. Steaks were placed into the cooler instead of greasy ground beef. Fresh items replaced canned. No more off-brands. Cakes that were hand-baked each morning arrived from gourmet bakeries, and nothing in plastic wrap or heavy in preservatives was prominently displayed.

All Andy had to do was look at his customers' faces to know that they were leaving happier and with better food than at any other time in the history of Johnston's Corner Market. At the end of each day, he felt confident that he had done everything in his power to provide the best food to as many people as possible.

In short, Andy was satisfied to think that the Corner would surely be a strong, serving, and central part of the neighborhood whenever the time came for him to offer the business to Stephen. And during the rare lulls in the store's daily activity, he found himself smiling gratefully and contentedly at the sight of the battered wooden door leading to the back storeroom where his grandfather—a young neighborhood grocer—had once slept.

CHAPTER FOUR

The Price of Progress

The First Cracks Appear

"They're saying it costs too much," Andy said to Stephen, who, despite the demands of the school year, was again coming to work with his father on the weekends to help handle the increased activity of the shop. "Here, listen to what this one says."

Holding the new September issue of *The City*, a popular news magazine, to the level of his eyes, Andy began reading aloud from its editorial section: "Through the course of its brief existence, Nourishaid has demonstrated its explosive growth potential as the number of voucher recipients continues to expand. Resulting from this expansion, the overall cost of operating the program is skyrocketing, with payments made to food providers already far exceeding any initial estimates.[10] In short, Mayor Ted Sprine and the city government must turn their full attention to managing cost control in any way possible, or risk the absolute runaway of the most crucial piece of legislation passed in recent Capital Springs history."

⑩ The Healthcare Connection: *Inflation Invades*

The already rapidly increasing costs of healthcare continued to rise throughout the 1960s and '70s, soon becoming a major concern in the United States. Rick Mayes describes the situation, stating that by "the late 1970s," the country became "marked by a growing national preoccupation with inflation, particularly in the area of health care" (37).

Stephen grimaced. "So what exactly does that mean?" he asked.

"I'm not really sure," Andy admitted, putting down the paper. "I thought everyone was really happy with the way things are going now. Plus, I assumed that if Sprine went ahead and passed this law and let so many people get onto the program, that he would have done his homework enough to make sure that the city would be able to afford everything."

"Yeah, talk about an oversight. That seems a little weird to me," Stephen responded as he began sweeping the linoleum floor near the front door.

"Well, this is just the magazine's opinion—nothing official from the government or anything. But they are using real stats and everything in the article," Andy pointed out. "I mean, I guess I can see what they're talking about. We're selling more and more to people with vouchers every day, and clearly the word is getting out, so I can understand how the whole thing might be starting to get expensive for the government."

Andy paused and looked around the still-crowded store, his gaze settling on a young man filling a produce bag with lemons before he continued. "But, like I said, I don't see how they can be so surprised by the outcome this quickly. I wonder just exactly what they thought was going to happen. I guess we'll keep doing what we're doing and wait to see if the mayor actually does change anything."

A Concerning Solution

Andy and Stephen didn't have to wait long, for within that same month, Mayor Ted Sprine announced that significant changes were indeed soon to come for Nourishaid.

In just a few moments, we will be passing you over to the mayor's office, where Mayor Ted Sprine will be delivering his address to the city. Andy and Stephen both sat at the front counter of the Corner and listened attentively to the radio, anxious to hear what the mayor had to say. With talk and rumors swirling through the media, everyone was eager to learn what the future of Nourishaid would—or wouldn't—be.

Good morning, Capital Springs, Mayor Sprine began. *As we press forward in our attempts to improve our communities, I am encouraged by what I see happening all over the city. With the passage of Nourishaid, the overall standard of living has risen, but there is work yet to be done. Many throughout the city continue to live in great need of the benefits this program has to offer.*

The initial success of the program, however, has not come without its price, as the actual cost of its operation has proven greater than originally anticipated. In addressing each of these pressing issues, I propose the passage of Article 223,® an amendment to the current Nourishaid program, which will expand Nourishaid eligibility to a greater portion of those still in need while simultaneously introducing measures aimed at curbing the program's rising costs. With this act, I believe we can move past these current obstacles and continue our drive toward a better, stronger Capital Springs.

⑪ The Healthcare Connection: *Additional Amendments*

In 1972 under President Richard M. Nixon, the nation passed the largest set of Social Security amendments in United States history. Key among these changes was Section 223, which added 1.7 million disabled individuals to Medicare eligibility, expanded eligibility to those with end-stage renal disease, and also attempted to place limits on what hospitals would be allowed to charge for Medicare patients' routine costs.

Also of importance was Section 222, which authorized the government to experiment using alternative methods of healthcare provider reimbursements, ultimately opening the door for the future transition to the Prospective Payment System (see Mayes).

"Huh, that sounds like an odd combination of things," Andy commented thoughtfully when the speech had ended, reaching over to turn the volume dial down. "How can we add more people to the system while at the same time cutting back on its costs? That doesn't make any sense to me." He furrowed his brow, frowning. "Both of those things seem to work against each other. I mean, if there's more people getting Nourishaid, that means more food, and that means it's going to cost more."

"You're right; I don't understand that either. I wonder what the new law will do to us?" Stephen mused. Then, with a shrug, he added, "Oh well. Either way, I've just got to keep cleaning floors and loading shelves, right Dad?" He laughed, standing up from his stool and heading to the storeroom.

Shortly after Mayor Sprine's speech, Article 223 was passed into law, and as a result, thousands more were added to the Nourishaid rolls. The new law expanded Nourishaid to include individuals suffering from severe food allergies and diabetes, making it easier for them to change and modify their diets, as well as to afford the specific foods they needed.

Article 223 also redefined what levels of income justified the need of aid, and as a result, a larger portion of Capital Springs's population began receiving food vouchers than ever before. All of this change was received with great excitement, as most people in the city praised Mayor Sprine's decision and celebrated the heightened level of security, protection, and care provided for the people by the city government.

It was the rest of Article 223 that nobody paid much attention to— the part that was intended to somehow decrease the amount of money it cost the government to pay for all this food that was now being eaten by so many people and stocked on so many grocery store shelves. The big change introduced by Article 223—the change that most people missed even as participation in the program expanded—was the fact that the government would now reduce its food compensation costs by reimbursing grocery stores only for those expenses that the government believed to be "necessary costs."

Essentially, as it reviewed the various expenses incurred by the city in compensating food providers throughout the city, the government had decided that many of the prices being charged by grocers were simply too high. These supposedly high prices, the city concluded, were responsible for the government's unexpectedly expensive Nourishaid operation costs. So under Article 223, anything deemed by the city to be an unnecessarily high cost would simply not be fully reimbursed.

The city's goal under Article 223 was to set limits on exactly how much grocery stores could charge for the food being purchased by Nourishaid customers, and then to enforce these prices throughout the city. The real difficulty for grocers in this new system sprang from the fact that the food provided to Nourishaid customers was not limited in any way, only the city's reimbursements for that food. When coupled with the continually broadening number of food voucher recipients, Article 223's new limits began creating difficulties for many Capital Springs grocers.

Frustrations Mount

"It's tough making this new system work," Andy tried to explain to Karl one evening after watching a couple leave the Corner, bags full of food in each hand. "Ever since Article 223, things have been getting a little bit difficult. I understand where the city's coming from and what they're trying to accomplish, but I think they're going about it the wrong way." He shook his head. "I'm starting to get a little worried."

"What do you mean?" Karl asked. "What did they do that's making it hard? I thought you and everyone else were loving Nourishaid."

Andy drummed his fingers on the counter in a slow, meditative rhythm. "Yeah, we were, and for the most part everybody still is," he began. "But the government's trying to change everything all of a sudden, and they're trying to save themselves money by basically ripping us off."

He straightened. "See, Article 223 says that grocery stores are charging too much for the food we're giving to Nourishaid people, so the city just decided that they're not going to pay us back fully—they're going to start deciding how much food is worth."

Karl still looked confused. "What? I don't get it—what do you mean? How are they ripping you off if they're setting the prices for food?"

Andy stroked his chin, thinking about how to make his predicament a little clearer to his friend. "All right, well, take that couple who just left as an example," he began, motioning toward the door. Looking down at the vouchers they had handed him before filing them away in the cash register, he continued, "Their final bill was seventy-eight bucks, fine, but now, when I submit this to the city, they turn around and tell me my prices are too high—that they're 'unnecessary costs,' and because of this, they won't pay me the full seventy-eight." Karl's eyebrows shot upward, which Andy took to be a good sign.

"They say instead that they'll pay me only something like sixty-eight because that's what the prices should be—that's what the city has decided is necessary for me to charge and for them to pay." Andy shrugged helplessly. "So really what they're doing is expecting me to keep providing the exact same food to everyone with vouchers, but without getting fully reimbursed. I think you can see how this could start getting tough."

Karl was nodding. "Yeah, you're right," he answered. "That definitely makes for an odd situation for you and all the other grocery stores."

"Basically, I'm just starting to get a little nervous about the whole direction this thing might start heading," Andy continued. He gestured toward the food-laden aisles. "Don't get me wrong; I'm glad more people are getting help from Nourishaid and that I'm able to provide food to so many of them. But the government can't start thinking they can save themselves money by simply not paying grocers back. Expanding the program while at the same time decreasing what they're willing to pay grocery stores would be the fastest way to make it hard on us all."

Karl didn't answer. He too was looking at the aisles dotted with shoppers, his lips moving soundlessly as though he were calculating just how much money a grocer could lose from their purchases.

After pausing to think for a moment, Andy resumed his monologue. "And another thing that really bothers me the more I think about it is the fact that Sprine is the one who messed this whole thing up to begin with. If he was going to start this program in the first place, then let more and more people get onto it, shouldn't he have planned it better? I mean, how can the whole government be so surprised by the outcome of Nourishaid—it's their idea to begin with."

He ran a hand through his hair, which was, as Karl knew, a sure sign of frustration. But Andy wasn't finished yet.

"Plus, instead of admitting a mistake and rethinking or reconsidering anything, the city just keeps giving vouchers to even more people so they can keep looking like they're saving the world, while behind the scenes, they start ripping us off by not fully paying us back. Sprine looks like a hero while I'm forced to take the brunt of his mistakes. It's starting to look to me like he's concerned only about saving himself!"

By this time, Andy was more than slightly irritated, and he forced himself to take a calming breath. "Sorry, Karl, I don't mean to get upset or anything. I'm just getting a little worried about what the city's trying to do here, you know? All I want is to keep doing what I've always done: try to sell good food to people and make enough for my family, and I don't want the government to get carried away with trying to save itself by making things hard on the people actually providing the food to everyone."

"Yeah, you're absolutely right," replied Karl. "That makes sense."

"Don't get me wrong," Andy added. "I'm totally fine and happy to keep going the way things are, and it's not like Article 223's going to kill anybody or anything, but I just want to be sure this whole idea of not paying grocery stores back for what they provide to people doesn't become a trend. I mean, no one can be effective at what they do in that type of a system."

He sighed and shook his head as he motioned one of his regular customers over to the counter.

"Things are good right now and a lot of people are getting a lot of great food," he concluded. "We can all be happy about that. I just don't want to see things get messed up, that's all—and this newest development is making me nervous.

"Well, hello there, Mrs. Marshall! How are you today?"

More Questions than Answers

By the time Article 223 had been officially implemented and the new reimbursements it introduced were being made to grocery stores, it was again December. Andy's walks between home and the Corner were accompanied by the soft fall of snow, and although it was cold, he enjoyed his journeys to and from the store because they were the only guaranteed free time he had each day to think. The cold weather meant that there were fewer people on the usually busy sidewalks, making it easier for his thoughts to flow freely.

It was amazing to him that after existing for only seven short months, the Nourishaid program had grown so much that it was now beginning to drastically change and evolve. Andy recalled the magazine editorial he had read to Stephen only a few months ago and realized that its fears of Nourishaid threatening to run away and become too much for the city to handle might actually be coming true—Mayor Sprine was certainly acting as if they were.

But how could the mayor not have known this would happen? Andy wondered morning after morning, his breath fogging the air in front of him as he walked. *How did the government not foresee this? Could their planning and figuring and estimating really have been that far off? Is it possible they really didn't understand how much food people would get when it was suddenly free to them? And then to let even more people into Nourishaid—how could they have thought that would help anything?*

There were no easy answers to these questions. The changes made to Nourishaid over the course of its young life had indeed led to a large number of voucher recipients, and this number only continued to grow as more families and individuals found themselves eligible for the program.

The swelling ranks of Nourishaid customers were using more food than the government could afford, and the reimbursement restrictions introduced by Article 223 had still not accomplished what Mayor Ted Sprine had hoped they would. Even after placing food providers in a difficult position, Article 223 was unable to stem the tide. Nourishaid operating costs continued to surpass the government's expectations, leaving Mayor Ted Sprine searching for a way to cut costs...somehow and somewhere.

A Worrisome Winter Holiday

The winter holidays proved to be a particular challenge for Andy, and by extension the Corner, as Andy attempted to reorient himself after the changes made by Article 223. As people throughout the city prepared for the visits of relatives and friends and began planning parties and dinners, the Corner was flooded with customers, many of whom were paying with Nourishaid vouchers.

Normally, Andy enjoyed the heightened activity and palpable excitement that the holidays brought to his store, but this year each new customer and each purchase added to his sense of foreboding. Because these were not ordinary parties or meals being assembled, it seemed that everyone wanted nothing but the best food Andy could provide, and plenty of it. By the time the holiday season had ended, Andy discovered that the Corner had suffered a significant loss on most of its Nourishaid customers.

"Apparently, Mayor Sprine feels that the city's grocery stores are charging unnecessarily high prices for the top-quality and specialty foods that Nourishaid customers are buying," he told Karl one snowy morning shortly after the new year.

"That doesn't make much sense," his friend responded, watching the flakes spiral lazily to the sidewalk outside. "Everybody knows that holiday foods are more expensive than your average everyday fare."

Andy sighed. "Well, you know that, and I know that. But I guess the mayor doesn't. In any case, the city has refused to compensate all of us grocers for the full price of the goods we provided."

Karl shook his head in silence. After all, what could really be said? The city's inadequate compensation had translated into a financial loss for the Corner. And what should have been a time of celebration and good cheer had instead been transformed into an uneasy time of worry for the future of Andy's family business and his livelihood.

Finding the Bright Side

Despite this new challenge, Andy's good nature soon bubbled up through his concerns. He brought himself to accept the present state of Nourishaid and Article 223 as something that was momentarily out of his control, and he decided that all he could do was to work hard with the best attitude possible.

If he had pulled the Corner through the grave trials of the city's past economic recession, Andy reasoned, he could certainly manage to survive the new difficulties facing him now. After all, he was ultimately providing food to more people than he ever had since taking over for his father, and at the end of a hard day, that was really what mattered. If he could provide a roof, a bed, and some food for his son, he was happy to simply be the reliable neighborhood grocer.

With these thoughts firmly planted in Andy's mind, the winter deepened and thawed, and soon the trees lining the sidewalk in front of the Corner wore the white blossoms of spring instead of the thick white frosting of snow. The changing season brought with it even larger changes for Andy, Stephen, and the Corner, since that May Stephen graduated from high school.

Happy with his latest accomplishment, Stephen looked forward to another comfortable and enjoyable summer working with his father. Since the number of Nourishaid recipients in Capital Springs had grown to include more than 20 percent of the city's population,[⑱] there were definitely enough tasks to keep both Andy and Stephen busy that summer.

⑫ **The Healthcare Connection:** *Medicare and Medicaid Advance*

By 1979, the number of Medicare beneficiaries rose to 28 million, and the number of Medicaid beneficiaries rose to 21.5 million. With a national population of just over 225 million, this meant that nearly 22 percent of the United States' citizens were now covered by either Medicare or Medicaid.

And, as they were soon to discover, the coming months would prove to bring even more changes to the Corner and to the way in which all of Capital Springs would receive its food.

CHAPTER FIVE

An Unfair Burden

It was another morning of what had become typical activity at the Corner. An ever-growing line extended back from the front counter where Andy rang up bills and bagged groceries as fast as he could, conscious that he had to quickly move on to the next antsy customer. Meanwhile, in between helping people find particular foods and pointing out correct aisles, Stephen hustled back and forth between the storeroom and various rows and corners of the store, attempting to restock all the shelves before the morning grew too late.

And as always, the radio provided a constant backdrop of various talk show hosts' tinny voices, all of whom were again discussing and debating Nourishaid: its strengths and weaknesses, its triumphs and failures. Because it concerned them so much, Andy and Stephen made sure to stay continually up to date with the news of Capital Springs and the Nourishaid plan's developments in particular.

Everyday Chaos

Food had definitely become an important concern for the city, and while everybody remained happy about the existence of Nourishaid, an increasing number of people were beginning to fear the rising costs of operating it. Article 223 had apparently not done enough to curtail the program's expenses, and both the number of people using food vouchers as well as the cost of funding the program continued to grow larger.

Alarmingly, because so many people had been allowed onto the Nourishaid rolls, even the amount of money the city was saving due to lower grocery store reimbursements was not enough to keep the program's costs down. Andy wasn't surprised that things were becoming expensive. He eyed the long line of customers, many of whom qualified for Nourishaid, waiting to pay for their food. *Somebody* had to foot the bill for their groceries!

The logical connection between an expanded program and rising operation costs seemed so simple and apparent to him that he just couldn't understand why neither the mayor nor the media seemed to understand the true nature of the problem.

The bottom line is that we, the tax payers; we, the very city of Capital Springs, cannot afford this program at the rate it's growing, and something has to be changed, said the voice on the radio. Andy barely stopped himself from rolling his eyes, which the customer he was helping probably would have taken amiss.

"Oh yeah, canned tomatoes are over on aisle three," Stephen answered a woman, pausing briefly from unloading a box full of egg cartons into the cooler.

Okay, okay, I think we all understand that this is just costing too much money, but let me ask you this: Would it work to just axe the program altogether? Just cancel the whole thing and start over again? the interviewer on the radio asked.

"Thank you for coming. Have a nice day," Andy said, quickly jamming the vouchers he had just been handed into the register and turning with a smile to the next person waiting in line. "Hi, how are you today?"

No, that is not an option, the radio show guest responded. *This program is essential to the growth and progress of the city. So many people in so many areas have become so dependent on Nourishaid that if any politician were ever to propose the disbandment of the program, there is almost no chance that he or she would ever be elected. It's just too late to cancel the program. There's no question that Nourishaid is here to stay—it has become an absolute necessity. What Mayor Ted Sprine needs to focus on now is simply cost containment and cost control in order to make the program sustainable.*[13]

[13] The Healthcare Connection: *Cost Containment*

The swelling rolls of Medicare and Medicaid led to large government expenditures, causing the government to become increasingly focused on finding ways to contain healthcare costs by the late 1970s. Consequently, President Jimmy Carter was forced to "subordinate his national health insurance proposal to an ambitious plan for containing hospital costs. The goal...to expand medical care and insurance coverage became eclipsed by...the urgent need to control health care costs" (Mayes 23).

The Corner was humming with voices and the sounds of activity. Stephen was answering questions, prying open cardboard boxes, and ripping open plastic bags, all set to the consistent tempo of the opening and shutting of the register's drawer. Andy's greetings to customers floated through the air over the dry roll of shopping cart wheels. Conversations and the constantly swinging front door overlapped. Amongst all of this, the voices on the radio held a constant portion of Andy's and Stephen's attention, and both waited anxiously for any semblance of free time so that they could continue their own discussions about Nourishaid, the city, the government, and the Corner.

Finally, a momentary lull in the day's activity allowed them to take a short break.

"It seems a little funny to me, too," Andy replied to Stephen, who had just sat down behind the counter with him and had commented on that morning's radio broadcast. "That's pretty much all anybody talks about anymore. Just getting control of how expensive it is for the city."

"I wonder what they'll end up doing," mused Stephen with a slight frown.

"Yeah, who knows? After Article 223 and changing everything on us all of a sudden, who really knows?" Andy shook his head. "All I can say is that if they keep trying to do more things like that, it's going to get pretty hard for all of us grocers, that's for sure."

"You're right about that," Stephen replied. Andy noticed that his son's hands were balled into fists. "I really hope they don't think they can just keep cutting back on what they're going to pay grocery stores every time they get themselves into trouble," Stephen finished.

"I know; I agree," answered Andy. "I hope they haven't set themselves a dangerous precedent. The whole thing's been kind of bizarre—I mean, first off, we signed up to try this new idea and when it all started everything was fine. We were happy just minding the store and making sure everybody was getting good food, and then all these other people and ideas from everyone outside the store started getting involved."

He shook his head at the injustice of it all. "After we're already on board and after we've done everything they've asked us to do with Nourishaid, they come along and start trying to control exactly how we run our store and telling us what the right costs for groceries should be—like they have any idea what they're even talking about."

No doubt about it—Andy was upset now too, and Stephen immediately piggybacked off of his father's rant.

"Yeah! If they're going to start a program and expect us to make it work for them," he continued, "then they should be ready to just let *us* make it work. Us, the ones who actually know what we're doing—not *them*! They've really messed things up by starting the program, getting everybody hooked on it, then adding even more people while all of a sudden trying to balance their budget by cutting the amount they're willing to pay us to run the thing."

He raked his hand through his hair, a gesture he'd picked up from his father. "I mean, we were getting food to everybody just fine without them deciding what the correct costs of food should or should not be. Plus, I still don't understand how they can expect us to keep giving away so much food if they refuse to pay us back for it all."

To that, Andy didn't have an answer.

Becoming the "Bad Guy"

The summer weeks continued to pass by, feeling shorter than usual due to the consistent busyness of the Corner. The warm morning walks from the apartment to work continued to be prized moments of the day for Andy and Stephen, for as soon as the shop opened for the day, customers began swinging through the front door and down the aisles, food began leaving in bags, and the shelves, stripped bare so quickly, demanded constant attention from Stephen, who restocked them each morning.

The radio's voices continued to speak and discuss until one morning the usual conversations were replaced by the voice of Mayor Ted Sprine himself.

I am glad to announce the continued success of the Nourishaid program, which is currently serving more citizens than ever before. It is truly flourishing, and we plan to ensure that the number of those receiving aid continues to increase. In making this growth possible, it becomes necessary for us to evaluate and consider our progress thus far, with particular attention paid to the sustainability of such an essential program.

In this vein, I propose the Financial Responsibility Act as a new and progressive model allowing for increased control of the city's finances, with a special focus on Nourishaid. With more than 20 percent of the city's population receiving some form of benefit from the food voucher program, this act will allow us to rein in the growing expenses of Nourishaid while enabling us to continue making the program accessible to more of those who need it.

Within weeks of this speech, the city had passed the Financial Responsibility Act[13] into law, and with it came more changes for Andy, Stephen, and the Corner.

[14] The Healthcare Connection: *Rethinking Reimbursements*

The Tax Equity and Fiscal Responsibility Act (TEFRA) of 1982 called for many reductions in federal healthcare funding, including a new system of *per diem* limits on Medicare reimbursements (for the sake of this analogy, weekly instead of *per diem* limits are used). Many of TEFRA's reimbursement cutbacks helped pave the way for the shift to the Prospective Payment System, which was soon to take place. The various measures and reimbursement restrictions of TEFRA "effectively sounded the official death knell for retrospective reimbursement" (Mayes 47).

The law's first point of action was to establish a weekly limit on grocery store reimbursements. Building on Article 223's idea of limiting the amount paid to food providers, the government set its limit at fifty dollars per family per week or twenty-five dollars per individual per week, and would not pay for anything beyond that, even if a Nourishaid customer's final bill did in fact exceed the limit.

Ostensibly, this plan would benefit all parties involved. The theory behind the Financial Responsibility Act, as outlined by Mayor Sprine, was that it would cost more than fifty dollars for some families to eat and less than fifty for others. Since the grocery stores could keep the difference if customers spent less than their allotment, it was expected that in the end, if grocers adequately managed their customers and their customers' food consumption, they could actually come out ahead financially.

Problem was, this new law now made it Andy's responsibility to somehow track and control the food-buying patterns of his customers. "Anything that exceeds the government's new weekly limits won't be compensated by the city," Andy explained to a concerned Stephen soon after he familiarized himself with the Financial Responsibility Act's details. "And if the Corner is to continue effectively providing food to so many people in our community, we've got to avoid any large financial losses. That won't be easy."

Immediately after the passage of the Financial Responsibility Act, Andy and Stephen began the difficult and sometimes awkward task of attempting to keep people's total bills within the weekly limits. They tried to help people understand that when they insisted on taking more than that from the Corner, they were actually forcing the shop to suffer a financial loss, which could eventually force the entire store to close down.

"If the Corner has to shut its doors, it'll make it harder for everyone in the area to get the food they need," Andy told each customer, hoping that they'd understand.

Ultimately, though, the only way to make people aware of the consequences of what they obtained with their vouchers was to explain the entire history and process of Nourishaid to them. And with lines of customers continually reaching from the counter toward the back wall, these types of explanations were out of the question.

Soon, Andy was repeatedly forced to make a difficult decision: Either he had to ask people to put some of their food back on the shelves—thus risking an angry confrontation—or just let them take what they wanted, understanding that his store, and therefore he and his son, would never be paid back for that bag of food.

"There's no way we can win," Stephen observed in a morose tone of voice one evening as he and his father walked home. "Either we're on the community's bad side, or we lose money. The city has us caught in the perfect Catch 22."

Stephen was right. Eventually, in an attempt to find a middle ground, Andy and Stephen attempted to provide only generic or off-brand products to their Nourishaid customers. "I hope this'll provide people whatever food they need while keeping *our* costs somewhere near the weekly limits," Andy told his son.

Unfortunately, the disappearance of many name brands quickly raised suspicious questions by both Nourishaid and non-Nourishaid customers alike. And when Andy attempted to explain the true impact of the Financial Responsibility Act and his endeavors to avoid the financial losses that it made nearly inevitable, he was answered by angry charges of selfishness and greed. The individuals making these accusations argued that he was attempting to lower the quality of food for Nourishaid customers in a profit-seeking ploy, and that increasing personal profit was Andy's only true motive.

In reality, of course, nothing had changed in Andy's feelings about being a grocer. He still loved the Corner and he appreciated the greater opportunities he now had to provide food to so many people living in the city he loved. But try as he might, he couldn't quite understand these new charges of selfishness. After all, beyond providing food to Capital Springs, the only other focus he'd ever had was simply to provide for his family…and he couldn't see why that would be called selfish.

Despite Andy's sincere attempts to explain the bind he was in to the Corner's customers, it quickly became clear that people were not willing to change their grocery shopping habits to fit the government's weekly limits. In fact, most of Andy's Nourishaid customers refused to take only their prescribed weekly allotment of food one week and return for another allotment's worth the next, or even to purchase anything other than their preferred brands.

"It's all too much of an inconvenience," one man explained to a dumbfounded Andy. "Plus, changing the way I'm used to shopping just doesn't make any sense."

The man paused and looked pointedly around the crowded store. "Why does it really matter that much anyway?" he added, leaning over the counter in an unmistakably aggressive stance. "Your grocery store always has plenty of business, and I'm sure you're making enough money already—why should the rest of us have to change our lives at all?"

Unfortunately, this incident was not isolated. Many of the Nourishaid customers who were new to the Corner accused Andy of being greedy and became angry when asked to comply with his new requests. Soon, he gave up his attempts to limit the Corner's new financial losses through appeals to his Nourishaid customers.

After a few weeks of this, the Corner was losing money on a regular basis. The number of people who had been allowed on the program, combined with the near impossibility of keeping Nourishaid customers within their weekly limits, caused Andy to become more anxious with each passing day. Specifically, he began to fear that real damage might be done to the store if nothing changed, and he decided it was time to discuss the situation with Stephen so that together they might come up with a plan to stop this trend of losses.

Fears and Frustrations

"We've got to fix this somehow," Andy told Stephen one evening after closing the store for the day. "If we keep losing money like this, we could be in real trouble—and what I'm talking about isn't really even about the money. It's about us just trying to do our jobs like we always have." He buried his hands in his pockets, trying to rein in his anxiously racing thoughts.

"You see, the crazy thing about all this is that if the Corner loses too much money, no one will be able to get food anymore, let alone all the Nourishaid customers! The bottom line is that I want to keep providing food to Capital Springs—to paying customers and Nourishaid customers both—but we can't do that if we're losing money every month. So, we've got to figure out some way to fix all this."

"It isn't right," Stephen agreed, his rigid posture betraying his anger. "Now we've got to fix these problems, and we didn't even start them. We've been just fine on our own since day one, since when Grandpa owned this place. Even Great-Grandpa apparently did all right—I mean, the shop's still here, right?" He kicked his foot repeatedly against the base of the counter. "I just don't see how we got stuck fixing all these problems that were other people's ideas to begin with."

"Yeah, that's true," Andy responded. He agreed wholeheartedly with his son's outburst, but he reminded himself that one of them needed to be the voice of reason. "That's definitely true...but for now, trying to fix it is all we really can do."

"Okay," Stephen said, letting out a long breath. "So what are you thinking?"

"I'm not quite sure," Andy admitted. "I *have* heard of some stores that are thinking about withdrawing from Nourishaid completely. You know, refusing to accept vouchers altogether. But I don't want to jump to that. Plus, from what I've heard, it isn't really a good idea anyway. The owners of other stores I know of who have been considering it seem to have realized pretty quickly that they just have too much of their business tied up in Nourishaid, and that it's not realistic to pull out now."

Stephen digested this as he got a broom out of the supply closet. As usual, the entryway was littered with leaves, bits of paper, and other debris that had swept in off the street during the day. "Well," he ventured as he began to sweep, "We could keep trying to get the people with vouchers to stick to their limits somehow."

He paused, looking at the big plate-glass window in front of him. "I know we've been trying to talk to people and explain things, but let's just make it an official store policy and maybe put big signs up or something. You know, so that people know what the deal is before they even come in!"

"Yeah, you know, I've been thinking a lot about that over the past few weeks," Andy said, nodding. "And in theory, I agree with you. But I've kind of realized that making all of the Nourishaid customers stick to that limit just might not work. For some people, sure—it's fine. But there really are a lot of them who honestly can't make it work."

Stephen looked skeptical, so Andy continued to make his case. "It's hard enough for a lot of our customers to get here, and who knows how much food they'll need when they finally do? And, really, it's not worth arguing over something like what brands people take. It does make some difference, but not enough to fight over."

Stephen resumed sweeping, but didn't say anything. Clearly, he still didn't agree, and so Andy pressed on. "Just the other day," he pointed out, "a really old couple came in here with vouchers. The husband had a hard time walking and he was moving slowly, using a cane. It took them a long time to get anywhere, and it looked like it hurt the guy to be walking around that much.

"Anyway, they didn't know about all the changes, and it's hard for them to get out of the house, so this was their one trip for the month. There really was no way for them to leave with only fifty dollars' worth of stuff and then come back next week for the rest—for them, it really wasn't possible. It really was too hard for them to get down here. I talked to them for a while, and it's amazing they made it here at all. So for them, I don't know if there was any real way to keep them at that fifty dollars."

"Yeah, that's true," Stephen answered as he walked back over to the closet to pick up the dustpan. "And actually, today I met a guy who's kind of like that, too. He was pretty young, and he had two real small kids in his shopping cart. He told me that he and his wife both work and that today was the only day off either one of them could get for the next three weeks, and so he needed to come get groceries for his family today. He was stocking up, and I guess it's like you said, for us to make them stick to only fifty bucks just wouldn't work.

"Making them come back for the rest next week wouldn't be possible either because of their work schedules," he added. "I mean, they must be going non-stop with work all day and then two little kids to take care of, too."

"Yep. The more I've thought it over, the more I'm starting to see how truly backwards some of this Nourishaid stuff is getting to be," Andy said with a sigh. "Obviously, the program is helping a lot of people, and like we always talk about, it's great getting to see so many people leave the shop with food in their hands."

He watched as Stephen stooped down with the dustpan in front of the pile of dirt and trash he'd swept up. "But I wish the government would solve their own problems, rather than throw them all on us."

Stephen grinned to himself, sensing that his father was gearing up for a long speech. He was right.

"If they start something like this, they've got to be sure they can handle it, but so far, every time things get out of control on their end, they just pass a new law and toss the problems back on us!" Andy exclaimed. "This whole weekly limit thing is doing nothing but punishing everyone involved—either we lose money and struggle to keep doing our jobs, or we crack down on everyone with vouchers, and they end up struggling to get all the food they need. Either way, it doesn't make sense."

As Andy continued to talk, Stephen dumped the dustpan's contents into the trashcan and rejoined his father behind the counter.

"How can we be punished for doing what we've always done and for providing people with food?" Andy asked. "At the same time, if we somehow make all our Nourishaid people stay under their weekly limits, then they're punished by receiving less food, which completely defeats the program's whole purpose. I mean, the people in need of the vouchers—the people this whole thing was started to help in the first place—end up pretty much the same way they were before Nourishaid even started: struggling to find the food they need.

"The whole problem here is that the government won't just rethink their ideas or admit they messed up, and so they keep trying to bandage it up by making us change everything and fix all their problems for them," he concluded, with more than a touch of bitterness.

Stephen paused a second before speaking, just to make sure Andy was finished. "Okay, so it sounds like we can't really change things too much with the Nourishaid people then," he replied. "What else could we do?"

A Plan for Survival

"I *have* been toying with an idea, but I need to see what you think," answered Andy. "I figure that if there's no way to make up for our losses with Nourishaid people—and the government won't help by doing the obvious thing and paying us back for everything we give—then the only other group of people we can change things with is customers who pay for groceries on their own."

"And what are you thinking about doing with them?" Stephen asked, hoisting himself onto a stool.

"Well, if we do our math, we can figure out exactly how much we're losing on Nourishaid," Andy said, pausing briefly and thinking before continuing. "Once we have that figured out, we can then try to balance it out by raising the prices of everything else in the store for paying customers."

Stephen's eyebrows went up, and Andy hastened to add, "I hate to do that, and I'm sure people won't be too happy, but prices change from time to time anyway, and we won't raise them too much—just enough to balance out our losses from Nourishaid."

"It makes sense, but do you think it's worth it? Won't everyone get *really* mad about that?" Stephen asked, still concerned.

"I hope not. I also know that most of the other stores in town are thinking about doing the same thing, or have already started to," Andy replied. "But I don't think we have too many options."

He held up one finger. "We can't very realistically force the Nourishaid customers to keep their limits," he said. "I feel like the people who have cooperated with us on that so far are probably the only ones who can. So that option's kind of out."

Andy held a second finger up. "There's no real sense appealing to the government since they're the ones who got us into this mess in the first place, plus they've already told us how much they're willing to pay us for the food we provide."

Finally, he raised a third finger. "There's really no other option but this third one. I'm hoping that if we make a small increase on the price of everything in the store, there won't be any big enough single changes to make people too angry. I mean, I think it's worth a shot—what about you?"

"Yeah, I guess you're right. I'm willing to do whatever you think is best, so if this is it, then let's give it a try," Stephen answered. "I'm just frustrated that the city has put us into this position at all. They keep getting more votes by expanding Nourishaid and making everyone feel good about the whole thing, but then they pay for it all by cutting back what we get paid—the money we need to stay in business. To top it all off, they leave us to be the bad guys who now have to raise our prices everywhere else,[8] and we're just trying to stay in business and keep providing food for everybody."

⑮ The Healthcare Connection: *The Cost of "Cost-Shifting"*

This is an important point in the analogy, and thus represents an important pattern in American healthcare policy. As politicians continue to expand healthcare programs, the costs of operating these larger programs naturally increase as well. Yet all too often, attempts at controlling these rising costs take the form of limiting the reimbursements made to healthcare providers. The combination of having to provide resources and services to an ever-growing body of patients while simultaneously receiving ever-decreasing reimbursements forces healthcare providers to incur financial losses. Attempting to counterbalance these losses, healthcare providers and hospitals often must raise prices for all other patients. This pattern, known as "cost-shifting," has become entrenched in American healthcare and is one of the largest factors explaining today's expensive healthcare prices. It will remain a prevalent theme throughout the analogy.

As he finished, Stephen stood up from his stool at the front counter and looked around at the store surrounding him.

Working here every day, Stephen felt he was beginning to understand the way his father saw things. This store was important to him. Selling groceries was important, not only to Andy, but to the entire community who bought their food here. And when the shop struggled or things didn't go well, it was up to Andy to guide the Corner through to safety. Now that he was more deeply involved with the shop and had begun to catch brief glimpses of exactly what it meant to be a grocer, Stephen hoped he too could help his father work his way through this current and most pressing struggle.

CHAPTER SIX

Enemy of the People?

Unaffordable Fallout

"I'm sorry, Karl, I don't know what else to do—I can't just let myself get run out of business."

Andy was trying to explain to Karl the reasons for the Corner's recent price increases, but with little success.

"All right, all right. Whatever you say." Karl held up a conciliatory hand. "But you've got to understand how this looks to people." He gestured to the store. "People like me, who have been shopping here all our lives. I just don't get why you're charging us more—it looks like you just flat-out betrayed us, and we don't really know why. You know people are going to be upset."

Andy sighed and tried to ignore the sick feeling in the pit of his stomach.

"Yeah, I guess you're right, but honestly, Stephen and I talked it all over, and we don't have too many options right now," he explained. "We're in over our heads, and we had to make a tough decision. It's just that Nourishaid has become so huge the government can't afford to pay grocery stores back fully—they've forced me to be the one who pays for the program—so I have to make that up somewhere else.

"I'm honestly not trying to be unfair or anything like that," Andy added as he watched his friend's expression, hoping against hope for a positive reaction. "I'm just really not sure what other options we have."

"Well, you do what you think you need to, but don't be surprised if most of us do the same thing," replied Karl. "Now that you've raised all your prices, a lot of us might not be able to shop here anymore, and we might have to go find somewhere else we can afford. I love coming here and I love you guys, but like you said, sometimes we have to make tough decisions."

Karl apparently *did* make such a decision, for Andy and Stephen began seeing him in the Corner less often. Unfortunately, Karl's reaction was a fairly common one for a large portion of the store's more regular customers. Many of them were people who lived in the neighborhood—people and families for whom Andy had provided groceries for years. Like Karl, the Corner's regulars felt that *they*, of all people, should be the last ones forced into making up for the shortcomings of Nourishaid. In fact, they felt that their years of loyalty to the Corner and to the Johnstons had been betrayed—and so, shortly after the price increases, many of them began searching for a store with lower prices.

Even as this shift occurred, though, Andy maintained a sense of optimism because he had the sense that his "regulars" would eventually be back. He explained his reasoning to Stephen one morning.

"You helped me to adjust the price of every item in this store," he began.

Stephen nodded.

"Well, so you know that we worked hard to ensure that our shop is still fair and comparable to others throughout Capital Springs, right?"

"That's for sure," Stephen muttered, thinking of the many late nights he and his father had spent to complete this task.

"The fact of the matter is, every other grocery store in the city is also dealing with the same issues that we are," Andy continued. "So as the Nourishaid program grows and stores keep struggling to counteract the losses they're sustaining from it, grocery prices across the city will rise—and I bet it'll happen quickly."

"That makes sense," Stephen said, nodding. "And hey—I bet that soon, Karl will understand what's forced us into this position."

"That's what I think, too," Andy responded, glad that his son had independently come to the same conclusion. "Once Karl sees that this situation is infecting stores way beyond the Corner, he'll come back."

History Repeats Itself

While Andy and Stephen were still attempting to deal with the fallout of these latest challenges, they were suddenly faced with a new change to Nourishaid. Mayor Ted Sprine and the city government announced another expansion of the program that provided vouchers to a larger group of pregnant women and children living in homes with low incomes.[16]

⑯ The Healthcare Connection: *Even More Expansions*

The Child Health Assistance Program of 1984 required states to expand their Medicaid programs to include a larger portion of low-income pregnant women and children.

Andy agreed that this was definitely a group of people who deserved the benefits of Nourishaid and was happy to help. He was surprised, however, to discover that no adjustments had been made to the fifty-dollar weekly limits. The individuals and families who had most recently fallen under the Nourishaid umbrella truly needed the best, most healthy food the Corner could offer, yet the government wouldn't change their reimbursement policies to make it more feasible for grocery stores to provide them the amount and the quality of food they needed.

Once again, Andy and Stephen had to make themselves accept the fact that they would begin losing even more money. The government was again expanding the program in order to improve its public image, and it was doing so at the expense of grocery store owners throughout the city.

Andy had long ago decided—and had taught Stephen—that their job as grocers was to provide people the best service they possibly could. Still, father and son alike couldn't help but feel that the city government was beginning to intentionally take advantage of them. Despite this feeling of betrayal, they refused to lower their standards, especially for this new group of women and children.

Just as Andy and Stephen had feared, though, when these new Nourishaid customers began shopping at the Corner, the store's losses only grew worse. The government still reimbursed the shop only fifty dollars each week for each family's shopping trip, and because there wasn't a single family with children that could realistically stay within that limit, the Corner continued losing money for doing nothing other than what Andy and Stephen had decided was their job and their duty.

Only one month after the introduction of this latest expansion to Nourishaid, Andy and Stephen were forced to again raise the prices on food sold to their paying customers in another effort to make up for their rapidly growing losses.

"All right, Johnston, this has gone far enough. You've got to stop it somewhere," lectured Mrs. Jameson shortly after the Corner's most recent price adjustments. She had moved into the area six years ago, and since that time had been a fairly regular shopper at the Corner. "I've shopped here long enough to know what your prices normally are, and I didn't say anything the first time you raised them. I believe in community, you know."

She nodded, as though to confirm her high-mindedness before continuing.

"But now, this is too much. I can build a community only with people interested in building the same thing, and if you're going to keep changing around all your prices and running the neighborhood all over Capital Springs looking for someplace else to shop—a place they can actually afford—then I may have to join them. I don't know if you think this is some clever way to make a little extra money or what, but you really need to think about what you're doing here."

Taking this to be a clear indicator of the general response to his attempts at balancing the Corner's financial losses, Andy once again decided that it was time to reconsider the shop's situation and, if possible, to devise a new plan of action.

Nowhere to Go but Forward

"Well, here we are again, Stephen, and just like last time, I don't know what to do," Andy said, exasperated. It was a Wednesday evening, and they had just closed the shop for the night. They were now seated at the front counter discussing what could possibly be done to help improve the Corner without causing a great deal of trouble for their customers.

"I know our price increases don't look good, but if people really knew what we were up against, they'd understand," replied Stephen, hoping to reassure his father. "I mean, is there even anything else we *could* do?"

"Unfortunately, I don't really think there is—not that I can see anyway," Andy said, shaking his head. "Last time we had this conversation, we kind of talked about the idea of dropping Nourishaid altogether, but now I know for sure we can't do that. I've heard of a few stores trying it, and they ended up getting right back onto it because it's become such a huge portion of their total business—they can't afford to lose all those customers.

"By now, even though we're losing money on Nourishaid, over half of the customers who walk through that door are on it," he continued, nodding toward the front of the store. "So if we all of a sudden got rid of all of them, we'd honestly lose such a huge chunk of our overall customer base that we'd have to shut down for good, just like those other stores found out."

At that, Stephen's eyes widened. *Has it* really *come that?* his dismayed expression was clearly asking.

"It's true," Andy told his son. "Look at everyone who comes in tomorrow and you'll see that too much of our business—of the store's lifeblood—is tied up in Nourishaid, so if we want to stay alive and keep providing food to people, then we have to stick with the program no matter what."

Both father and son were silent for a few moments, contemplating the rock and the hard place between which they were wedged.

"And all that's without even mentioning our role in the neighborhood," Andy continued, his voice sounding loud in the otherwise silent store. "Even if we could afford it, I don't know how I could feel good about just cutting all those people off."

"So does that mean we just keep raising prices if we can't find anything else to balance ourselves out with?" Stephen questioned.

"It's really looking that way. I can't see any other way out of this thing—we really are in over our heads."

Smiling tiredly at his son, Andy stood up, and, after switching off the lights, the two of them emerged into the refreshing darkness of night, glad for the chance to temporarily remove their minds from the difficulties of the Corner, and headed toward home.

Another Adjustment to the Status Quo

Before that week was up, however, Mayor Ted Sprine announced yet another major change to Nourishaid, this one focusing entirely on the government's reimbursement policies for food providers. Following the trend of earlier changes and amendments to Nourishaid, this new bill was passed into law not long after the government's most recent expansion of the program.

According to the official statement issued by the mayor to the city's grocery stores, Nourishaid was now to operate under the Probable Cost System,⑰ which would entirely change the way in which Nourishaid costs were assessed and paid to grocers. The government would no longer reimburse grocers based on the amount or type of food actually taken from their stores. Instead, the PCS's new method of payment would be based on the dietary needs of each Nourishaid member.

⑰ **The Healthcare Connection:** *Readjusting Reimbursements*

The Social Security Amendments of 1983 called for the transition of Medicare reimbursements to the Prospective Payment System (PPS) under which healthcare providers are compensated according to patients' particular Diagnosis-Related Group (DRG). This change was implemented in October 1984, and the final transition to PPS rates was completed in Fiscal Year 1988 (see Dafny).

Through a series of surveys and questionnaires, those receiving food vouchers would report their individual diets, lifestyles, and needs, after which each Nourishaid member would be assigned to a particular category that would include others with similar circumstances and needs.

The government's board of food distribution experts had apparently been studying dietary health and the overall economic trends of food consumption throughout Capital Springs, and had compiled a complex classification system through which every person using food vouchers would be assigned a particular category. Each category had a reimbursement rate attached to it, so that now, rather than pay grocery stores based on the actual costs of food and customers' final bills, the government would pay a flat rate for each customer according to their Probable Cost System classification.

As usual, most Capital Springs citizens had no real knowledge of these changes and directed no thought toward understanding how they might impact the overall process of food production, distribution, and consumption within the city. As far as Andy could see, the general population was content with their ignorance—no one really wanted to think about all the messy paperwork and behind-the-scenes formalities grocers had to deal with. Most people continued to treat food as an automatic part of life, as a given, without considering exactly how it found its way onto their tables and into their stomachs.

Along with the official statement introducing grocers to the Probable Cost System, the government had delivered a book with detailed descriptions of the program, as well as boxes of new forms and paperwork. One morning, while Stephen began his usual task of restocking shelves, Andy was again—for the third time—reading through his official copy of the "Probable Cost System Food Provider's Manual" and flipping through its accompanying pile of paperwork in an effort to become better acquainted with all the new customer classifications, the proper way to file paperwork, and any other details about his role in this new form of Nourishaid.

To Andy, the new system seemed like a labyrinth whose walls were ten feet tall and provided no clues for navigation. There seemed to be an overwhelming number of Nourishaid customer classifications, each of which had even more subcategories beneath it in hopes of accounting for any possible variations in people's health, financial circumstances, family size, dietary needs, age, and on and on.

Setting the manual down and running his hand through his hair in frustration, Andy looked up from the counter. "This is ridiculous," he said loud enough for Stephen, who was then busy in the produce section, to hear. "I don't get this classification stuff. It's as if they realize people can't really be classified into nice and neat little categories, so they came up with a million different slight variations, but in the end, they're still just putting people back into categories.

"There's no way this could ever work out right," he added. "I mean, everyone's got completely different lives going on and everyone eats slightly different stuff. The cost of food itself fluctuates from time to time. I just don't get it. It all seems too complicated a way to get people fed."

Andy was right—selling food and operating the Corner became a much more complex, and at times confusing, process after the introduction of the Probable Costs System. Now, not only did Andy and Stephen have to do their usual work, but they became burdened with the new and formidable task of constant paperwork. In fact, Andy soon found himself spending more time sitting at the desk in the back room completing paperwork while Stephen attempted to take over the register, in addition to the regular restocking of shelves and general maintenance of the shop.

The headache didn't end there, though. The actual filing of PCS paperwork presented another challenge, for if any detail of a form was filed incorrectly, the government would send it back to Andy to be corrected and resubmitted before any compensation was provided. Sometimes, the errors were so minute and obscure that they were virtually undetectable, and these corrections often took Andy nearly as long to complete as his initial attempt to file the first piece of paperwork.

In the process of filling out paperwork, submitting it to the city, allowing time for the city to review everything, finding it to be incorrect and therefore returned, figuring out what went wrong, completing the paperwork again, resubmitting it, and finally waiting for the city's review of the corrected paperwork, the Corner often received no compensation for weeks. And occasionally, lost in the hectic shuffle, forms were simply forgotten about and payments never received.

"I feel like I'm living in the Land of Paperwork," Andy complained to Stephen one evening during their walk home. "But completing mile-high stacks of forms and files isn't even the tough part."

"That's not surprising, given the government's track record with Nourishaid so far," Stephen replied as they waited for a traffic light to change.

"Yeah. See, whether or not a customer's actual food bill falls within or beyond his allotted reimbursement rate of his particular PCS category seems to be a game of chance," Andy explained just as the light turned green. "Some people *easily* stay within their category's payment rate, but other people go way beyond. So if a person takes less food than the PCS category allows for, then the Corner earns a profit."

"That'd be a welcome change," Stephen interjected.

"Sure, but if a customer's final bill is higher than the PCS allotment, we suffer a loss. And I don't know which way the pendulum's going to swing."

A Familiar Face Returns

After the second month of this new system, it seemed clear that the Probable Cost System had failed to make any significant changes or improvements for food providers. Despite making small profits on occasional Nourishaid customers, the Corner's overall trend of financial losses continued, and Andy's concerns about the welfare of the Corner persisted.

It eventually became necessary for Andy and Stephen to once again raise the prices of food for paying customers. They did so apprehensively, but as before, felt that this was the only way to ensure the Corner's survival as a neighborhood grocery store that provided food to so many people.

A short time after increasing the Corner's food prices, Andy and Stephen were surprised to see Karl come strolling through the shop's front door.

"Hey, guys, how's it going?" Karl called across the entryway. "It's good to see you again, and you'll be happy to hear that I'm coming back as the good old faithful customer, and not only as your friend."

"Yeah, good to see you too," Andy answered with a smile. "Look, I'm sorry if I did anything to make you feel bad about not shopping here anymore. I want you and everyone else around here to do what's best for them. We're here to be sure we all eat, and if you've got to go somewhere else to do that, then I understand..."

Karl held up a hand, putting a halt to Andy's apology. "Thanks, Andy, but don't worry. You handled everything just fine. I'm starting to see what you're talking about—things are getting kind of crazy these days."

"What do you mean?" Stephen asked, joining them at the front counter.

"Well, I know you guys have had to raise your prices a couple times now, but that exact same thing is happening all over the city. Everyone's raising and re-raising their prices," Karl answered. "Believe me, I know. I drove to every store I could find, and everywhere it's the same thing. Food's getting pretty expensive anywhere you go in Capital Springs, so I figured maybe I was the one being a little hard on you guys."

At that, a small smile appeared on Stephen's face. Karl clapped a hand on his shoulder. "You tried to tell me you were doing what you had to just to keep this place alive, and I should have listened," he admitted. "But anyway, I figured it's time to come back and support the neighborhood and my friends a little bit more, especially since it's becoming so expensive everywhere else in the city. Plus, you two are actually doing really well with your prices compared to some others that I saw, so overall, I'd say you're doing an amazing job with all of this."

Karl's assessment proved to be accurate, and soon—just as Andy had predicted—the rest of the Corner's regular customers also began returning. Everyone had the same story: Prices on food were becoming so expensive everywhere they went that it no longer made much of a difference where they shopped, and so they decided it would be best to stay in the neighborhood and buy their food at the Corner.

Even Mrs. Jameson began shopping at the Corner again, although somewhat grumpily. She was now convinced that all grocers throughout Capital Springs were working together, somehow conspiring to take advantage of the situation in order to gain larger profits. Still, she had to eat, just like everyone else.

Payment Plans and Purpose

Unfortunately, the common spike in food prices throughout Capital Springs introduced a new and startling problem. Many individuals and families who did not qualify for Nourishaid benefits, and who had previously been able to purchase their own food, now suddenly found themselves unable to do so in the face of rising prices. As a result, there were many who were forced to either go without all the food they needed, or attempt to find some alternative method of payment.

Faced with this new challenge, some grocers were willing to work with their hard-pressed customers, providing temporary fixes such as discounts, payment plans, and purchases on credit. On the other hand, there were many grocers who felt they could not afford the added liability of such actions in addition to the losses already incurred by Nourishaid. In fact, many stores began sending struggling customers to their competitors who *were* willing to make alternate arrangements.

Andy and Stephen decided immediately to be one of the shops willing to work with needy customers, which came as no surprise to those who knew them well. As the weeks dragged past, the Corner began receiving many new customers whom neither father nor son had ever met before. They were all struggling to afford enough food and had been sent to the Corner by other grocers in the hope that Andy and Stephen would arrange some way for them to obtain what they needed.

"Hi, are you the person to talk to about possibly doing payment plans or something like that?" a young man, who appeared to be in his mid-twenties, asked Stephen one afternoon while he was working behind the front counter. Andy was in the storeroom trying to catch up with PCS paperwork.

"Yeah, sure, me or my dad."

"Okay, well, my name is James," the newcomer said quickly, shaking hands with Stephen. "I was just over at Appleton's and they told me I should come here and talk to you guys."

"All right, that's fine. What can we do to help you?" Stephen asked, even though he was pretty sure he already knew the answer.

"Well, I'm really sorry about all this," the young man began. He was clearly uncomfortable, and his gaze darted toward the door as though he'd like nothing better than to dive back through it. "I recently graduated from college and then pretty quick after that I got married, and, well, my wife and I are really struggling to get by—we're just starting out, you know what I mean? We both work, so we don't qualify for Nourishaid, but at the same time, we really can't afford these expensive food prices. We feel like we're kind of stuck."

"Congrats on college and the wedding and everything," Stephen said enthusiastically, ignoring the bad news for a moment. "That's great."

"Hey, thanks," James replied, looking somewhat relieved by Stephen's friendly reception. "So, like I said, I tried to see if the guys at Appleton's could work something out with me, but they said they couldn't, and then told me to talk to you. I'm not looking for anything free. I'm just looking for some way I can get what we need right now and then have some time to pay it all off while we try to get our feet beneath us. Do you think you could help us out at all?"

"Yeah, I think we can work something out," Stephen answered with a firm nod. "Hang on one second; let me go talk to my dad."

Stephen left James standing at the counter for a few minutes while he related to Andy everything he had been told. Re-emerging, Stephen told James it would be fine for him to shop and to get whatever he and his wife needed. Furthermore, he'd be welcome to shop at the Corner anytime, and as long as he needed to, Andy would allow him to keep a running tab, provided that James and his wife made a minimum payment on their balance each month.

While this would mean that the Corner would incur a short-term loss while waiting for their full payment, at least James and his wife would be able to get whatever food they might need. Trusting that the shop would eventually be repaid in full, Andy and Stephen were glad for the opportunity to help another customer who genuinely needed it.

"Thank you so much," James said after hearing Stephen's report. "You guys are really saving us, and we're more than happy to pay any type of interest or whatever you need us to. You're just helping us out so much right now by letting us get this food."

"You're welcome," replied Stephen. He was more affected than he wanted to let on by James's obviously heartfelt thanks. "And don't even worry, my dad and I don't accept interest. Just pay us back whenever you can. Everything will be fine."

After James had filled a shopping cart and left the shop, Stephen again felt he was beginning to more fully understand his father and exactly what the Corner meant to him. *Regardless of how difficult things become*, thought Stephen, *this is the type of thing that really matters. This is our purpose.* He felt content and happy after seeing the difference he and his father had made in the lives of two people they didn't even know.

It was this type of experience that proved to Stephen just how meaningful being a grocer could really be. It was certainly not some grand business scheme—the Corner's financial plagues and his father's frantic efforts at conquering a mountain of paperwork seemed to demonstrate that. Being a grocer was something essential to life and to the happiness of the entire city.

This passing back and forth of customers unable to afford the rising prices of food continued as a regular practice, so much so that it was soon given a nickname. As food distribution continued to be a consistently important issue of debate and discussion both in the political world and in the media, the term "customer dumping" was finally coined to describe this newest phenomenon in the world of food providing.[18] The shuffling around of customers became a troubling trend compounding the difficulties brought about by Nourishaid, for it represented a new portion of the city's population now unable to keep up with the rapidly inflating cost of groceries.

[18] The Healthcare Connection: *The Death of "Dumping"*

The practice of sending patients with no form of healthcare coverage to other hospitals or healthcare providers willing to treat them became known as "patient dumping." This played a key role in subsequent healthcare policy, eventually leading to the passage of the Emergency Medical Treatment and Active Labor Act of 1985.

Finally, the summer that had brought so many changes began to approach its end as Andy and Stephen attempted to balance the everyday duties of operating a grocery store, handling Nourishaid customers, completing piles of paperwork, and focusing on the newest task of working out and keeping track of alternative payment methods for non-Nourishaid customers in need of assistance.

Pin the Blame on the Grocer

Capital Springs was once again entering another autumn season with its orange afternoons and cool evenings. It was only two years ago that Mayor Ted Sprine won his campaign for re-election, and since then, so much had changed for Andy, Stephen, and the Corner. Andy was fortunate to have had Stephen with him in the shop each day during the past summer. He enjoyed working with his son, and as life as a grocer continued to change in unexpected ways, he was certainly grateful that Stephen had been there to help.

How differently would things have turned out if Stephen hadn't been there to keep the shop running smoothly while I tried to understand and adjust to the ever-changing laws of the city government's food distribution program? Andy wondered. He was glad he hadn't had to find out.

In the second week of October, an early snow fell, dragging with it to the ground many of the multi-colored leaves of fall. The morning of the snow, Andy and Stephen walked quickly to reach the indoor warmth of the Corner and after settling in discovered the news.

"Whoa! Hey, Dad, come look at this," Stephen exclaimed, holding that morning's newspaper above his head. "Looks like this might be something big. Have you heard anything about this?"

"What are you talking about? Which article?"

"Here, this one: 'Sprine Announces Major Shift in Food Policy.' Read it, quick."

Stephen stood back and watched his father's eyes as they shot rapidly back and forth across the lines of text. When he finished, Stephen asked again, "Have you heard anything about this? What's the Emergency Food Provision Act?"

"I don't know," Andy said as a feeling of trepidation crept over him. "This is the first I've ever heard about it, but from what the article says, apparently they're going to try to fix all the customer dumping that's going on. I have to say, though, I'm a little confused by the parts talking about the new emergency category and a law making all grocers provide food to anybody who comes through their doors. You're right, this sounds big. We'll just have to wait for more information, I guess."

The Emergency Food Provision Act[19] was indeed shaping itself into a significant piece of food distribution legislation, and, later that afternoon, Andy and Stephen listened to the radio as it broadcast Mayor Ted Sprine's official announcement of the bill and his pleas for its immediate passage into law:

Good afternoon. It is with great excitement that I speak to you today in order to call for the speedy passage of the Emergency Food Provision Act. I believe that this act will prove to become the next crucial step in our march toward progress.

Too many of our grocers are now working against the city's program of food distribution and are therefore contributing to the persistent funding problems continuing to plague Nourishaid, and now the entire city. Too many of our grocers have no stake in our communities—in our people— and have stepped beyond the bounds of all ethical principles in the name and pursuit of exorbitant profits.

By repeatedly raising the price of food and refusing to lower it, grocers throughout Capital Springs are creating a new food crisis as people citywide are struggling to afford the elevated and greedy demands of grocery store owners. Most recently, many stores have begun the practice of customer dumping, sending hungry people away empty-handed simply because they are unable to afford the rising cost of groceries.

No person in this city should ever go hungry and without food. Eating and having access to food are basic human rights, yet too many grocers refuse to provide food to those in need for no other reasons than monetary ones. The passage of the Emergency Food Provision Act will put an end to this by outlawing the practice of customer dumping.

With this act, all grocery stores will be required to provide food to any individual in a state of food emergency and therefore in dire need of immediate assistance. Grocers must provide this food assistance regardless of the individual's income or ability to pay. This will ensure that more of those truly in need of food and its nourishment will find it—an act that will finally place our city on the right track for improvement, moving us out of the exploitative and profit-seeking shadow of the self-serving grocer.

⑲ The Healthcare Connection: *Financial Loss to Save Lives*

The Emergency Medical Treatment and Active Labor Act (EMTALA) of 1985 requires, among other things, that all hospitals that participate in Medicare and that operate active emergency rooms treat all individuals seeking emergency care. EMTALA's passage effectively ended "patient dumping" and required hospitals to treat any and all emergency room patients (see "Key Milestones in CMS Programs"). As highlighted in the analogy, under EMTALA, hospitals are now required to treat all patients, regardless of their ability to pay for the treatment received. Since many individuals lack any form of healthcare coverage, whether private or government-sponsored, a large portion of emergency resources that will never be reimbursed are used in treating these patients. This is yet another significant source of financial loss that hospitals must recoup elsewhere, typically by raising the prices of services to other patients.

After hearing the mayor's speech, Andy and Stephen stared at each other in disbelief, feeling hurt, confused, and angry. How had they become the monsters? The bad guys? What did Mayor Sprine mean about "grocers have no stake in our communities" and "pursuit of exorbitant profits"? All of this was something new to them. Something that went far beyond the passage of laws and the changing of policies—this was a manipulation of fact; a calculated discounting and twisting of the lives and efforts of three, even four, generations of the Johnston family, along with every other grocer throughout the entire city.

"Does Mayor Sprine think he knows better than us how to run a grocery store?" Stephen burst out, not even bothering to keep his voice down. "Does he know, or even stop to *consider*, how the Corner's been trying, *really* trying, to make everything work and to keep the people of the city well fed? Does he consider the amount of food that we're just *giving* to Nourishaid customers, never to be fully compensated?"

Stephen slammed his palm onto the counter, drawing the glances of several customers. He wasn't finished yet, though.

"And what about the various individual arrangements we've made with people like James to make sure that they don't go hungry?"

Andy looked at his agitated son and agreed with him completely. "I don't know, son. The mayor kept talking about 'emergency,' but I think the only reason the entire city isn't *already* in a complete and total state of chaos is us—the grocers. We've been bending over backwards to keep things running at all. And now we're the ones being framed as the cause of the so-called 'emergency.' I just don't know what to make of it."

Lost in these questions and thoughts, Andy attempted to push back the stinging in his gut and in his mind, and to prepare himself for another day, another week, another month, another year of trying to sell groceries to a city demanding his services while making it increasingly painful to do so.

Why am I even doing this? he wondered—a question that would occur to him more and more often as time went by.

CHAPTER SEVEN

More Wrongs Don't Make a Right

"Free Lunch" Becomes a Reality

Mayor Ted Sprine's urging soon came to fruition as city officials gave the Emergency Food Provision Act, or EFPA, their vote of approval. The enactment of this new law, aimed at providing food to non-Nourishaid individuals struggling or unable to afford the cost of groceries, had significant effects on food distribution in Capital Springs.

Most immediately noticeable was the end of customer dumping. No longer could stores choose to send customers away for being unable to pay for their groceries. Instead, every grocery store was now required by law to determine whether or not an individual qualified as "in emergency."

In implementing this new law, the government defined an "in emergency" individual as one who, due to financial restraints, had consumed fewer than ten full meals in the previous five days. If this were the case, the individual in question was legally considered to be "in emergency," and any grocery store in Capital Springs would then be required to provide that person whatever groceries he or she needed with no questions asked and no requirements for payment, either then or in the future. Of course, the grocery store could *ask* for payment...

and even try to collect its fees. But, in the end, the customer who was "in emergency" was essentially under no obligation to pay for the food he or she received.

In typical fashion, this new act was praised throughout the city as another example of progressive leadership and insightful action, while the impacts it would have on the actual food providers—and eventually all the citizens of Capital Springs—were largely ignored.

The pivotal point of the EFPA was the fact that ultimately no one was responsible for *ever* paying the grocers back for the food given to "in emergency" customers. Since these people were not on the Nourishaid rolls, the government had no responsibility for compensating grocers for the food given, and since they were deemed "in emergency," it was assumed that by definition they were unable to pay for the food themselves.

The law, according to Mayor Ted Sprine and city officials, was aimed at ensuring that the city's growing population of non-Nourishaid residents would never run the risk of going without food because they had no ability to pay. Rather, these residents would continue to have access to food without being pushed from one store in Capital Springs to another. The opinion that grocery store owners were operating out of a selfish desire to increase profits became the prevailing thought throughout Capital Springs, and any previous customer dumping or changes in grocery prices were held as proof of the accuracy of this argument.

It was only logical, therefore, not to worry about who would actually be paying for EFPA emergency food. As long as the government's costs to operate Nourishaid didn't rise as a result of the law and more people were gaining access to free food, the majority of the city felt that the desired goal was being accomplished. The grocers would cope as they always had; besides, they all had more than enough food on their shelves at any given moment to feed anybody coming through their doors—so why shouldn't they be required to feed those who were struggling to eat, free of charge and without compensation?

Despite the general attempts of the city to ignore the full scope of the EFPA's effects on food distribution, the impacts of this new law could not be kept hidden for long.

One evening in early November after closing the shop for the day, Andy and Stephen were working together on finalizing some lingering stacks of PCS paperwork. In reviewing the shop's recent activity, they realized that during the previous week, nearly 10 percent of their customers had claimed emergency status under the Emergency Food Provision Act and had consequently left the store with groceries for which the Corner had never been and would never be reimbursed.

It struck both Andy and Stephen as odd that suddenly Nourishaid, which had already introduced significant financial losses through its inadequate reimbursement schemes, had now suddenly become their much more preferred government food distribution program. At least with Nourishaid, some of their costs were covered, whereas nothing at all was covered or compensated with EFPA customers.

"I know there have been times in the past when we thought it was hard to keep up with all these new laws, but it's never been this bad," said Andy, a note of genuine alarm in his voice. "The EFPA is just going to kill us—that's all completely free food we're giving away—all of it is a 100 percent loss for the store. We can't take hits like that too often and still hope to come away alive. Nobody can."

"I know. I'm completely blown away by how many people are coming in and filing themselves as emergency cases," responded Stephen, leaning back in his chair and stretching his arms above his head. "When it was first passed, I could understand where Sprine was coming from, but now that I'm seeing it in action, I can't believe it. How can anyone in their right mind expect every store in the city to just give food away on a regular basis? You're right; nobody can survive this if it goes on for too long."

"The thing that really gets me is all this talk about us being selfish and greedy," continued Andy, gathering up the papers that were scattered across the desk. "It seems like nobody understands what's really going to happen if the government and everybody else keep stretching us too thin. What's going to happen is that we're all going to be forced out of business, and then *nobody* will be able to get food very easily.

"I mean, this all originally started to get more food to more people, but the way it's going now, we're heading toward the exact opposite, and I feel like I'm no longer being allowed to do the job I love and to do my best to get food into the homes of this city."

Sighing, Andy began to file the papers in their proper folders and drawers. "And one last thing: How is it that the grocery store owners became the only people in the city responsible for feeding everyone all the time? If the city wants this, shouldn't they do their part and be willing to actually pay for it to happen properly?"

Unattainable Goals

Under the new rules and requirements of the EFPA, every grocery store began feeling the same pressure. The combination of inadequately reimbursed Nourishaid expenses, together with the new weight of entirely uncompensated EFPA expenses, meant that grocers throughout the city were losing more money than ever before. And consequently, they were forced to continue raising the price of food for every remaining paying customer. Not surprisingly, the city became angrier and more frustrated. People lamented the high price of food, and the debates over what more could or should be done to fix the city's food distribution system raged wildly.

Not only did the population feel they were being charged too much for food purchased with personal money, but they also felt that Nourishaid, in its current state, was consuming too much of the city budget. Paradoxically, however, many city officials, with the support of the city's residents, continued attempting to broaden the program to include even more people with even more food benefits. In attempting to both reduce its costs and expand the program, the grocers were the ones stuck in the middle, forcibly stretched, twisted, and contorted in order to fit the demands of poor governmental planning and a discontented public that at times seemed insatiable.

As the upheaval continued, Andy tried to believe that the politicians who were finding new ways to give away groceries had only the best of intentions. However, when the evidence was so clear that their actions were ultimately responsible for driving up food costs and thereby making the city's food problems even worse, he began to question what was going on and why all of this was happening repeatedly with no sign of improvement for anybody, provider or consumer.

The days and weeks passed, and more changes to Nourishaid continued to be made. To Andy's dismay, each one increased the number of food voucher recipients while failing to make reimbursements to grocery stores any more adequate.

"It seems to me that Mayor Sprine is specifically identifying particular groups of people to include in the program," Andy mused one morning after he and Stephen had finished listening to the morning's radio broadcast. "And as time goes on, of course, a larger number of individuals and families become eligible for vouchers. They begin receiving benefits that entitle them to more groceries and higher quality food."

"Yep, nothing new there," Stephen replied, wondering what his father was driving at.

"Here's the thing," Andy said, pointing an agitated finger at his son. "There've been all these changes and increases to how much food grocers must provide, but there *haven't* been any accompanying changes to the Probable Cost System's grocer reimbursement rates! You realize, of course, that this means—once again—we grocers are going to be forced to provide more food to more people, without being compensated any differently."

Andy, of course, was right, and the latest string of Nourishaid changes only served to contribute to the trend of grocery store losses. In fact, many began scrambling to find ways to limit their losses simply to remain in business.

In the Crosshairs

Months slumped past, food prices rose, and the city's anger over its food distribution system grew. Despite not fully reimbursing the grocers, government officials continued to talk about the unnecessarily high cost of operating the Nourishaid program, especially after its multiple expansions to include more people and to provide more benefits.

Along with the government's seemingly endless complaints about the cost of food distribution, the general public of Capital Springs was also angry over the higher prices they were now having to pay for their own food. This was a direct result of the costly impacts that the ever-growing Nourishaid program and the EFPA were having on grocers, but very few citizens knew or cared about these "details."

With so much frustration in the air, the anger of the city formed itself into one large beam, like a searchlight, which swung this way and that before finally coming to rest on the grocers—the people actually providing the food demanded by everyone.

"I can't believe this!" Andy said hotly one afternoon, switching off the radio behind the front counter. "Everyone's all over us now!"

After listening to a full hour of talk show hosts and other people throughout the city rail on grocers as the root of all the city's current food problems, Andy couldn't listen anymore. The general argument had become focused on debating the efficiency or inefficiency of the city's grocery stores—*not* the ill-conceived governmental programs that were the real problem. A constant flood of Capital Springs residents, often led by government officials, criticized the city's grocery stores for not offering their products for more reasonable prices.

After all, the voice of Calvin Michaels, one of the city's popular radio talk show hosts, barked over the front desk of the Corner one afternoon, *the food prices in our neighboring cities and towns always seem to stay within reason. So why can they do it but our grocery stores can't? Why not start holding our grocers accountable for what's going on in this city?*

On top of these criticisms, and to the shock of Andy and grocers elsewhere in Capital Springs, Nourishaid received nothing but praise. Mayor Ted Sprine received credit for initiating much-needed progressive reforms, and now talk was beginning to focus on what new actions he might take to really begin the fight against high food prices.

"I'm so tired of hearing this stuff," Andy continued. "We hear it on the radio, we read it in the papers and magazines—that's all everyone's talking about! And we're always the ones made out to be selfish, greedy monsters!"

He clenched his jaw briefly in frustration before continuing.

"They keep talking about our insanely high profits, like we're all millionaires or something, but we're mostly just concerned with keeping our doors open. I really can't believe it. Can't anyone put the pieces together and see what's going on around here? Sprine and the rest of this city's government are forcing us into this!"

Apparently, no one *was* able or willing to put the pieces together, because Capital Springs's frustration over food prices continued to grow more intense. And in less than a month, it became inevitable that some form of action would be taken by the city government. It was a cold and clear morning in late December, and Andy and Stephen had just settled in for another day of work when the radio brought to the ears of Capital Springs the latest announcement from the mayor's office:

It is imperative that we work to decrease the overwhelming cost of food in this city. While it is true that more people are eating than ever before, getting enough food continues to be a trial for many, both within the Nourishaid program and increasingly without. We must work to repair the damage being wrought by unscrupulous and profit-seeking businesspeople within the food distribution industry who have unreasonably continued to raise prices, and by so doing, have forced us into a general food crisis.

With this in mind, I announce a significant and much-needed adjustment to Nourishaid's Probable Cost System. This adjustment serves as the first step in our new commitment to battle rising food costs by reducing the payments made to food providers in all PCS categories by 1.22 percent.[20]

This will open the window for Nourishaid to more effectively serve the people of this city as we embark on our journey toward making food available and affordable to all citizens.

㉒ The Healthcare Connection: *Disproportionate Inflation*

Entering the 1990s, healthcare costs rose at double the overall rate of inflation, and in 1990 the Health Care Financing Administration (HCFA) reduced all Diagnosis-Related Group payment weights by 1.22 percent, resulting in a $1.13 billion decrease in annual healthcare payments (Dafny 1532).

"Another change, another blow to us," said Andy after the mayor's speech had ended. Staying optimistic was just too difficult; he simply felt defeated. "Doesn't the mayor know there's nothing else we can do? When he keeps reducing payments to us after increasing the number of people covered by Nourishaid, we have no choice but to raise our prices to everyone else even more. I hate doing it, but especially after the EFPA, we have absolutely no other options. But I guess that people's reactions can't get too much worse than they already are."

After the lowered reimbursement rates had gone into full effect, the Corner's losses did in fact become worse. Andy and Stephen raised their prices for the rest of their customers. People became angrier.

A short time later, the government decided that the Nourishaid program needed to be expanded yet again, this time to increase its coverage of families with children. The amount of food each of these families was entitled to receive increased, but the reimbursement rates to grocers remained at the same low levels, failing again to account for this latest growth in the amount of food grocers were required to give away.[20]

㉑ The Healthcare Connection: *Increased Care for Children*

In 1990, the government introduced a new program to fund the cost of childhood vaccines and to provide compensation for those suffering from adverse reactions to vaccinations. The Budget Reconciliation Act of 1993 similarly initiated a new child immunization program.

Working hard to keep pace with the latest series of changes to Nourishaid, Andy often wondered at the way in which the grocery business as a whole had changed since he first took over the store from his father in what seemed to be just a few short years ago.

"Sometimes I barely recognize my own job anymore," he told Stephen. "Now I spend so much of my time and effort at the Corner on things that didn't used to be part of providing food." He ticked off the list on his fingers. "Paperwork, files, reports, reading manuals, and keeping up with the changes in the city laws. I'm sorry, Stephen, but if I'm able to pass the Corner on to you, I'm afraid you'll have to spend more time on administrative stuff than you do stocking shelves, sorting produce, or helping customers."

Paperwork Prevails

As the winter continued, the beginning of the new year brought with it a flurry of activity. The government quickly initiated a new act focused on the administrative side of Nourishaid. The Food Providers Accountability Act[22] required grocery stores not only to continue the lengthy process of filing customers' category information in order to receive their payments from the government, but also to keep more detailed and specific customer data such as the tracking of dietary needs, recording what types of food were purchased in each visit, and other eating habits and trends of each individual customer.

[22] The Healthcare Connection: *Double-Edged Data*

The Health Insurance Portability and Accountability Act (HIPAA) of 1996 required new levels of patient data security. This led to additional administrative costs for healthcare providers and opened the door for future abuse of healthcare tort law.

With all the paperwork now accompanying each and every Nourishaid member, the Food Providers Accountability Act was primarily intended to ensure that all personal information became more accurate and thorough, as well as being kept completely private and secure, confirming that nobody besides the actual customer and the food provider knew any of the details regarding one's dietary situation. All of this was accomplished through a rigid set of data recording and filing procedures, in which the slightest errors were to be punished with heavy financial and legal penalties.

Now, more than ever before, Andy considered in dismayed awe the ways that being a grocer had entirely changed. The age-old profession of providing food was becoming a legal procedure, a transaction no longer involving human beings. It was instead a complex web of paperwork, documents, and reports. With this new legal threat casting its menacing shadow over the Corner, Andy often felt that being a grocer was no longer about the food at all.

Following the Food Providers Accountability Act, the city government passed yet another bill into law. This one entitled disabled individuals who were attempting to find jobs to the full benefits of Nourishaid.[23] By now, a huge portion of Capital Springs's elderly, retired, unemployed, disabled, sick, pregnant women, children, and low income families and individuals were receiving food by means of the program.

[23] The Healthcare Connection: *An Incentive to Work*

In 1999, the Ticket to Work and Work Incentives Improvement Act (TWWIIA) expanded the availability of Medicare and Medicaid for certain disabled beneficiaries returning to work.

The grocery stores were busier than ever as the EFPA now required them to provide food to essentially anyone who walked through their doors, regardless of that person's ability or inability to pay for the food taken. And, of course, the government continued to demand more from the city's grocers while continuing to refuse to help them in their efforts by failing to provide adequate support or full compensation.

Because of this, the Corner struggled financially. Andy and Stephen both agreed that they'd like to hire someone with the skill and training needed to accurately file paperwork and handle the legal side of Nourishaid, but they knew they couldn't afford the extra expense. So on what often felt like the verge of madness, they scrambled to complete these additional tasks on top of the already demanding job of running a busy grocery store.

And at the height of their frantic efforts to keep the doors of the Corner open every day, Andy and Stephen came crashing into a high wall, fifteen feet thick, and built of bricks.

Skewered by the System

One afternoon, while Stephen literally sprinted between restocking shelves, helping customers, and bagging groceries at the cash register, and Andy struggled through piles of paperwork in the back room, the Corner was visited by Sandy Samuels, attorney at law.

Ms. Samuels came on behalf of a man named Clifford Jacobsen, who had recently recovered from a bout of food poisoning after buying groceries, including a pork roast, from the Corner. Jacobsen, who had only recently recovered from his unfortunate weekend, was determined to sue Johnston's Corner Market for what Ms. Samuels informed Andy was known as "food malprovision," arguing that their food was the cause of his pains.

"Whoa, hang on a minute," Andy said, interrupting Ms. Samuels mid-stream. He stood up abruptly from behind his small desk, the top of which was buried beneath a stack of papers. "I know for a fact that nothing he could've bought from this store was bad when we sold it, so it must be something he did afterwards, or food he got somewhere else.

Did he leave it out too long at his house? Did he cook it right? Did he get food at another store?"

"Mr. Johnston, I am simply here representing my client and communicating his position," Ms. Samuels coolly replied. "He is prepared to take this issue to court, but is also willing to make a reasonable settlement outside of the courtroom. That is his offer."

Andy's hands balled into fists. "How can he be the one controlling this situation and making me offers?" he demanded, the volume of his voice slightly rising in anger. "I know for a fact we did nothing wrong—we check everything we sell and pull anything off the shelves that's past its sell-by date." He took a deep breath and looked the attorney in the eye. "So I guess Mr. Jacobsen can try whatever he wants to, but I'm not going to be bullied around for something like this."

"Very well, have a nice day. But before I go, here is a statement issued by the district court granting me access to all of Mr. Jacobsen's customer files." She handed the slip of paper to Andy, who read it quickly and thrust it back in her direction.

After thumbing through his drawers of files, fuming all the while, Andy finally retrieved the paperwork for Clifford Jacobsen. He had no idea who this man even was, and as indicated in his customer report, he had shopped at the Corner only once. Andy handed the papers over, and with that, Sandy Samuels turned on her heel and left the building.

Exactly one week later, she returned.

"My client's position has not changed, and he remains prepared to sue your company for food malprovision. After reviewing his files, it appears that you have also failed to properly record Mr. Jacobsen's allergy to pine nuts as part of his PCS classification," Ms. Samuels said stiffly, as if delivering a memorized speech. "Under the Food Providers Accountability Act, may I remind you of the penalties for such an oversight, and of the fact that if he so desires, Mr. Jacobsen has every right to sue for this as well?"

Andy fought back a surge of panic.

"Fortunately for you," Ms. Samuels continued, "he remains willing to reach an agreeable settlement outside the courtroom, and, in light of this glaring error," she held up Jacobsen's customer file, "it would be wise to consider his offer. I will return in one week's time for your answer. Good-bye."

By the time the week was up, Andy had been forced to consult a lawyer, Mr. Simpson. And to his dismay, he and Stephen had learned that Ms. Samuels did in fact have a compelling argument. According to Mr. Simpson, even if the courts were to throw out Mr. Jacobsen's claims about food poisoning, he could still show that the records were not perfect and therefore imply that Andy and his store had been negligent in the performance of their legal responsibilities as food providers.

"Even though it's likely that you haven't done anything wrong," Mr. Simpson warned, "given the current atmosphere of anger against grocers, it's unlikely that a jury would side with you after hearing that there was indeed an inaccurate filing of customer records and PCS categorization."

"But the filing didn't have anything to do with his food poisoning!" Andy exclaimed for what seemed to be the millionth time. He had run his hand through his hair so many times that it was now standing on end.

"That is not the point," Mr. Simpson answered, pursing his lips. "If you take this case to court, you run the very real risk of losing a substantial sum of money. It is not a matter of what you did or did not do. It's a matter of what they can make a jury *think* you're responsible for. If they see that you miscategorized Mr. Jacobsen's PCS file, they will have questions about other things as well, and, in the end, it will leave you in a poor position…possibly even worse than the one you're in right now."

As he heard this explanation, Andy became increasingly dismayed. "So I'm required to first off allow this guy, Mr. Jacobsen, into my shop, then provide him with essentially free food under Nourishaid, *then* keep and file huge amounts of generally unrelated paperwork on every subject from apples to zebras in order to keep track of every aspect of this program that usually won't pay for the cost of my food. And then, after all that, Mr. Jacobsen's attorney can scour all my records, find some unrelated, inconsequential clerical error, and I could end up losing in court?" Andy asked, entirely exasperated.

"Generally, yes," Mr. Simpson replied.

"So how is any of this right or fair to me, and why does this make me want to provide food to anybody anymore?" Andy questioned under his breath to himself. Despite his continued conviction that he was in the right, though, it seemed that an out-of-court settlement was his best option.

And so, much as it galled him, Andy met with Ms. Samuels—now accompanied by Clifford Jacobsen—the following week. In the course of their meetings, it came out that, yes, Clifford had indeed eaten the pork extremely undercooked, and that, in all likelihood, this was the cause of the food poisoning.

For an instant after this confession, Andy thought he was saved. But the issue of the paperwork remained, and, in the end, Andy was forced to settle with Clifford Jacobsen for $9,000, a third of which went directly to Ms. Samuels. For a small neighborhood grocer already struggling to hold the weight of the city, this was a staggering amount and possibly a fatal blow, considering that it came in addition to Mr. Simpson's fees.

After this latest struggle, things began spinning faster and faster. Andy felt that his head was continually being drawn first in one direction and then another by loud and unfamiliar sounds. As soon as he looked toward one startling sound, another, more unnerving than the first, caused him to start, jerking his head in the opposite direction. All this noise and turning and spinning was tiring to Andy, and there were days now when his only desire was to lock the Corner's front door, hurl the key as far as he could into the dark and snowy night sky, and sleep, never thinking or feeling anything about food again.

"The worst part of the whole ordeal is that we don't even know the guy," said Andy despairingly as he and Stephen walked home after the unpleasant episode had finally ended.

"Yeah, it's bad enough that we didn't even do anything wrong, but we've always been so focused on being a good, solid neighborhood store!" Stephen responded, full of righteous anger. He kicked a sizable clump of snow into the street. "We used to know everyone who came through our doors, and we were part of the community, you know, but now that's all gone."

"Exactly," Andy said. "I can't believe this guy just came in here, walked away with our food, and then came back and completely forced us into settling up with him for all that money—for not doing anything wrong! I don't know how we'll recover from this." Andy's head hung and he passed his hand slowly over his closed eyes.

"I'm sorry about all of this, Dad," Stephen said, stepping forward and embracing his father. "I'm so sorry. You're working hard, and doing so much. I'm so sorry."

Feeling tired and beat up, Andy allowed himself to be held by his son for a few moments before they resumed walking. As always, on these days when Andy wanted to simply surrender the Corner to the night and leave, it was Stephen who pulled him back to reality and to hope. Stephen had always pulled him back; even as a tiny child unaware of the full meaning of his mother's death, he was there to bring Andy back to reality.

With his eyes closed, an image of Stephen emerging from the back storeroom with some box or bag of food played through his mind. This quickly faded into a memory of his wedding day and Jessica's smile, which was succeeded by an image of the storeroom that his grandfather—Stephen's great-grandfather—had once called home while working to build his store out of an empty space with one glass window.

All these images and thoughts rushed together in Andy's mind, and he remembered that since his grandfather's time, Johnston's Corner Market had become a living, breathing piece of the city and the neighborhood. This was the place where friends and neighbors had so happily come for food, where they greeted each other with smiles. This was where Andy had once worked with his own father—the place where he learned the importance of a passionate life, even for small corner grocers.

During the citywide recession, this had been a natural meeting place for the neighbors to gather when things were tough, when jobs were scarce, and the cold of winter was made worse by the freeze of failure and the threat of bleak tomorrows. Andy remembered that single mother and those dented cans of food. He thought of her grateful smile, and, years later, he still smiled in response.

This was the place from which Andy had watched Capital Springs recover and become happy once more. This was the place to which he, Andy Johnston, walked through the brisk morning air each day with his son, Stephen Johnston, to ensure that this living piece of Capital Springs continued to breathe its vital breath into the life of their neighborhood.

Remembering all this, Andy once again found a determination to continue selling groceries and to provide his community with the best food he possibly could. He would continue, and, somehow, the Corner would recover...wouldn't it?

CHAPTER EIGHT

A City Forever Changed

Crisis Mode

Three months had passed since the Corner's collision with Clifford Jacobsen, and the store continued to limp along. By now, the burdens placed on grocery stores throughout Capital Springs had grown heavy enough to collapse walls, and many stores in the city had indeed closed their doors and gone out of business. The demands were too much, and the support far from adequate.

As grocers attempted to balance the losses incurred by so many Nourishaid and Emergency Food Provision Act customers, as well as the many layers of restrictive government actions, the overall cost of food for the city's entire population continued to skyrocket. At the same time, Nourishaid had grown and expanded so quickly that the government continued to find it difficult to make the meager payments they did provide to grocers. In short, the city struggled to afford the system it had created. Everyone remained upset and frustrated, and it had become common to refer to the system of food distribution within Capital Springs as simply a "crisis."

This crisis reached into the lives of all within the city as, despite Nourishaid's multiple instances of expansion, there were still many deeply indigent citizens who went without. Those paying for food on their own also struggled to afford increasingly expensive groceries. And at the heart of it all, the grocers—the individuals and the stores providing the food lifeline for the entire city—had to contend with the forced losses of empty reimbursements, unnecessary lawsuits, restrictions, rules, laws, codes, paperwork, and continual ridicule as selfish, greedy, and evil profiteers.

With all this chaos swirling around them, Andy and Stephen were grateful still to be selling food, and they were glad to see the Corner every morning despite the fact that it was moving through each day with a pronounced limp. At least it was still breathing.

New Leadership, Same Problems

Another election season had come and gone, and, not surprisingly, food was the most pressing and concerning issue of the campaign. In another close contest, Mayor Ted Sprine was finally replaced by Stride Pen, who many considered to be the most charismatic and progressive candidate for the mayoralty that Capital Springs had seen in decades.

Throughout his campaign, Pen had made food distribution reform a top priority, and his vows to address the high cost of food by passing new laws aimed at making groceries available and affordable to everyone in the city had ultimately led to his election. The city anxiously awaited his inaugural speech to hear exactly how he would approach the food issue and just what actions he would attempt to take first.

At last, the expected day arrived, and Andy and Stephen, while restocking shelves and working through mounds of paperwork, joined the rest of Capital Springs by turning on their radio. As the new mayor began to speak, the entire city listened:

This is a momentous day in my life and in the life of the city of Capital Springs. I thank you all for your votes, and I vow to work my hardest to live up to the promises I have made and the expectations you have of me as your mayor.

Capital Springs has seen a great deal of growth and change throughout the past years—some good, some bad. As I begin my term of service to you and this city, I will make it my focus to build upon what positive progress we have experienced while also working to eliminate any negative consequences we may have encountered in the past.

In accomplishing this, I will focus on enacting much-needed reforms to our city's food distribution system. While Nourishaid and other laws such as the Emergency Food Provision Act have opened the doors to many, there are still those among us in great need of such services.

Compounding this problem, and even more pressing, is the rapidly and continually rising cost of food everywhere in the city. It is this which has created the largest trial for our people as the vast majority of those who work and strive to support their families now find themselves struggling to do so as a result of exorbitant food prices. The extreme profit-seeking of unscrupulous food providers has for too long placed the desire for wealth over the needs of our people, and it is time this trend is reversed.

"Here we go again," Andy said to Stephen, interrupting the sound of the new mayor's speech. "We know this routine all too well." Turning back to the radio, he continued listening:

In the past, Nourishaid has repeatedly made efforts to find an appropriate level for food costs, yet obtaining food remains a challenge for far too many. I promise to work with the city council to create a government-run system designed to meet the food needs of all residents of Capital Springs. Only when the food distribution system as a whole is managed by our city's government will we be able to ensure that all people have access to the food they require.

I believe that if current Nourishaid reimbursement rates were to be mandated as grocery prices across the board for all people—whether receiving Nourishaid benefits or not—food would reach an affordable level for every person and every life circumstance. We have an obligation to ensure that food is provided for all—indeed, what greater responsibility could we have to ourselves and our communities?

Finally, as I look beyond our borders, it pains me to see that every other city in our region has lower grocery costs than does Capital Springs. Our food is no different, our people no less worthy, so why is it that our grocers demand so much more than those in our neighboring cities and towns? I will work to provide answers to these questions, and, in so doing, pledge to bring the heyday of profiteering grocers to an end. As your new mayor, I promise to finally place people before profits, and to bring our food crisis under control.

"It's just what I was afraid would happen," Andy concluded, shaking his head as he turned down the volume. "A new mayor, but the same results—expand the program, decrease the payments, and blame the grocers."

"How is it that nobody seems to understand what's happening here?" Stephen asked. "We're still the monsters. We're still the cause of the problem, while all we're doing is just what we have to for us to keep opening the doors of this place every day. If the grocery stores get forced out of business, *nobody* will have food."

"Yeah, you're right," Andy said. "I don't know how much more of this the city can take. How much more we or the Corner can take. Just look at how many grocery stores have already shut down."

He was silent for a moment, chewing the inside of his lip in thought.

"I don't know how much more we can take," he repeated, his voice dull and solemn.

The Tide Begins to Turn

By the end of Mayor Stride Pen's first month in office, his various ideas, reforms, and promises became organized into a single bill, which he quickly proposed to the city and the city council. News of the possible law again reached Andy's and Stephen's ears as they paused momentarily from another day's work to listen to the mayor's voice streaming from the radio's speakers:

As previously promised, this new act, which will be known as the Food Cost Balancing Act, will provide food for all Capital Springs residents and will continue compensating grocery stores at the current Nourishaid reimbursement rates, officially establishing them as the standard for food costs regardless of how the food is being purchased or who is paying for it.

Through this, the government and all individuals will pay the same price for the same food, thereby ensuring that the needs of all our people will finally come first. The day of profit-mongering food providers and grocers will have reached its end. I therefore urge the city council, all city officials, and the people of this good city to approve the official passage of this groundbreaking legislation as soon as possible for the benefit and health of us all.

After Mayor Pen's new ideas had been officially announced and the city had had time to think through his proposals, Andy and Stephen were surprised to hear that for the first time a portion of the city was beginning to question if this were really the best route. It was true, though: As the proposed Food Cost Balancing Act was further examined and discussed, a significant voice of opposition was raised.

Many people began asking the questions that Andy and Stephen had been raising for years, wondering if perhaps the already thick layer of laws, bills, acts, amendments, expansions, and changes that had been made to the city's system of food distribution hadn't in fact become the very root of their current problems.

"Finally!" Andy exclaimed one morning after reading an editorial in the newspaper. "Finally, there are other people here in Capital Springs who are beginning to realize that maybe the government has created its *own* problems, not us grocers."

"I know!" Stephen replied. His voice held a note of enthusiasm that hadn't been there in months. "This is great. And did you see the end of the article? The author points out that if Nourishaid and the other government-operated food programs are already failing to provide affordable groceries to people, then how is putting the entire food industry under this same faulty program possibly going solve their problems now?"

"It seems that Capital Springs is finally starting to see the light," Andy responded with satisfaction. It turned out that Andy was right—more and more questions about the efficacy of the current food distribution program were raised, and this new voice of opposition continually grew stronger.

Meanwhile, Mayor Stride Pen doubled his efforts to push his law through the city council's vote as quickly as possible. He began daily campaigns in various neighborhoods of the city, during which he made speeches decrying the grocers of Capital Springs while praising the ingenuity of his proposal.

For many, however, the mayor's efforts raised even more doubts. They wondered why he seemed so personally intent on passing the law, especially when it became clear that the city's population now understood the real issues and was not in favor of this proposed change. Did the mayor not intend to listen to their concerns? Did he not intend to answer their questions?

"I can't believe how hard he keeps pushing this law," Stephen commented to his father one afternoon after reading about the mayor's latest speech in the newspaper. "He also really likes this new attack he's making on us grocers, doesn't he? I guess he thinks that the more he can attack us for something, the more people will listen to his ideas."

It was true; in his attempts to bolster support for his Food Cost Balancing Act, Mayor Stride Pen had begun leveling a new complaint against the city's grocers. Almost since the creation of Nourishaid, accusations of greed and selfishness on the part of grocers had been common, but now the mayor went out of his way to draw comparisons between Capital Springs and other surrounding cities.

In these comparisons, he described the food distribution systems of other cities as flawless and perfect programs, better in what sounded like every way than that of Capital Springs. (Interestingly enough, though, Mayor Pen never specifically named the cities that had developed the "perfect program." Rather, he simply referenced the "other cities" in general.) According to his speeches, these aforementioned "other" cities were able to feed their citizens all the food they would ever need without any real problems, while Capital Springs stagnated beneath unaffordable prices and inaccessible groceries. Mayor Pen argued that the only reason Capital Springs was unable to do as well as its neighbors was because of the extreme inefficiency of its grocers.

"Yeah, that's for sure," Andy commented. "We *are* operating inefficiently, but not for the reasons the mayor thinks. He keeps talking about how all the food here is so expensive while every other city around us is virtually giving their food away. But, of course, that's only half the story."

"No kidding," Stephen said over his shoulder as he worked on restocking the aisle closest to the counter.

"I think it's interesting that Mayor Pen never mentions the fact that those other cities actually have much lower quality food and fewer choices than we do, *or* that grocery stores in other cities have only a fraction of all the regulations and legal stuff to deal with that we do," added Andy. "He just tries to make it sound like they all have some sort of magical source of free food, but what's the good of telling everyone their food's free if they don't really have anything that great to give?"

"Mayor Pen aside, though, it sure is nice to hear people starting to understand the other side of the argument," said Stephen as he returned to the counter. "Although Pen keeps trying to make us the monsters, at least there are some people out there who are now realizing what's really happened around here. I mean, it's such a relief to hear people finally talk about the way we've all been forced into this whole mess. I've even read a couple articles lately that have gone so far as to say it's a miracle we still have food at all."

Stephen's entire face was animated now. "One guy even wrote that without the hard work and smart thinking of grocers, the entire food industry could have fallen apart. With people starting to understand what's going on, I'm not sure why the mayor keeps pushing this kind of change so hard."

Stephen was right, for as Mayor Stride Pen bore down on the city with constant campaigning, the voice of the people continued growing louder in response. The mayor described the Food Cost Balancing Act as the only possibility for solving the city's battle against unaffordable food prices, and the more these speeches continued, the more the people questioned him. The citizens of Capital Springs had apparently heard enough campaigning and began calling for the city government to lessen its involvement with the food distribution industry. Many wondered what would happen if everyone simply stepped back and allowed the grocers to figure out how to provide food on their own, without the constant involvement of the city government.

It soon became painfully apparent, however, that the mayor was fully set on achieving his desired outcome. Nothing, it seemed—not even the clear disagreement of many throughout the city and on the city council—could dissuade him. Many of the radio discussions heard in the Corner were now focused on Mayor Stride Pen's relentless drive to ensure the passage of "The Mayor's Law," as the Food Cost Balancing Act soon came to be known.

The conversations being broadcasted included political analysts arguing different sides of the issue. Many believed that after winning the mayor's office through an avalanche of lofty promises, Mayor Stride Pen needed the successful passage of this law to provide a sense of legitimacy to his term as mayor; in other words, he needed to prove to the city that he could in fact deliver on the promises of improvement upon which his entire campaign had been built.

On the other hand, it was argued that many of those within the city who opposed The Mayor's Law had been misled by incorrect information being disseminated by the grocery stores themselves. Mayor Stride Pen, these people argued, was thus demonstrating outstanding leadership by risking his political future in order to do the right thing, even if it was unpopular.

As the day for the city council's vote drew near, there was a great deal of doubt surrounding whether or not the bill would have enough support to pass. In the midst of the final campaigning efforts for the potential law, opponents of Mayor Stride Pen began accusing him of using unfair tactics to ensure votes from council members. They claimed that the mayor was attempting to buy votes with promises of political favors, and the most adamant of the mayor's opponents even accused him of simply threatening to destroy the careers of the council members who did not vote in favor of his food reform law.

The Final Nail

Regardless of accusations, theories, suspicions, speeches, rallies, and debates, the day of the city council's vote finally arrived, and Mayor Stride Pen watched proudly as the Food Cost Balancing Act was voted into law, winning a favorable outcome in the city council by just one vote.[23] The next day, surrounded by a group of his most loyal campaigners and advisors, the mayor signed his name to the bill, officially declaring the Food Cost Balancing Act as law.

[24] The Healthcare Connection: *Dubious Reform for America*

On March 21, 2010, with a 219-to-212 vote, Congress approved President Barack Obama's sweeping healthcare reform, designed to overhaul a great deal of the nation's healthcare system. Much attention was paid to the reform's promises of greatly cutting healthcare costs and expanding coverage to over 30 million uninsured Americans (see "United States Healthcare Timeline").

The following week, Mayor Pen delivered one more speech to the city in praise of this newest law. Andy and Stephen paused briefly from their work to listen to the mayor's voice as it was broadcast throughout the city:

The recent passage of the Food Cost Balancing Act will prove itself to be the most progressive, most meaningful act of legislation this city has seen since the very inception of Nourishaid, and will forever change the way this city receives its food. In reaching this pinnacle, the road has certainly not been easy. Many in the city have become skeptical and critical. Many doubted us and said that meaningful progress could never be made. They said the city would fall apart if we passed this law, but I am here today to invite us all to look around.

We are still here, the sun rose this morning as it always has, and the city is now poised to reach a new height of strength, stability, and security. Refusing to give in to the doubts, pressures, and criticisms of the naysayers, we are all finally on our way to truly ensuring that everyone in this great city has access to food. Now I ask you, what can be better or more significant than this?

Andy turned to face Stephen and, with the trials, losses, and heartaches of the past weeks, months, and years running vividly and painfully through his mind, said, "He really has no idea what he's done—it's impossible to know just how expensive food is until it's free. Now how will anybody eat?"

EPILOGUE

Consequences

Closings Commence

The winter had turned the world a solid gray by the time Andy and Stephen became the last grocery store in the neighborhood. In fact, Johnston's Corner Market had become the last grocery store still selling food within a five-block radius, and doors continued to close on more dark and empty grocery store buildings throughout the city.

In implementing the recently passed Food Cost Balancing Act, Mayor Stride Pen and the city government had begun enforcing Nourishaid reimbursement rates as the standard price for all food in the city. These mandatory lowered prices quickly took their toll on grocers throughout the city, and, in just a few months, the burden of having to sell all groceries for the already-too-low Nourishaid rates proved far too heavy for many to overcome.

The first big scare was Corley's. Andy personally knew Jake Corley and was familiar with the success he had enjoyed. After opening a small shop with his brother as a young man just out of high school, Corley had managed to expand his business to include five large stores scattered throughout the city. When all five of them suddenly closed, Andy became extremely worried.

"I don't know what to think. If Corley can't handle it, this is serious," Andy said on the morning walk to the Corner after hearing the news. Stephen had become accustomed to hearing a note of worry in his father's voice, but today that note was deeper than it had been; this was a note approaching fear.

"This makes it clearer than anything else," Andy continued as they trudged through a layer of wintery slush. "Pen's new laws are too much. I mean, there were stores already going out of business just trying to deal with Nourishaid and EFPA, and that was back when we could still charge normal prices to some of our customers."

As he spoke, his breath fogged the air in front of him in angry bursts.

"But now that we have to sell everything in our stores for the impossibly low Nourishaid prices, it's too much to handle!" he added. "The government is making us provide food to the entire city for prices lower than what the food is really worth. They're forcing us to operate at a constant loss—a loss worse than anything we've seen before!"

Andy and Stephen walked the rest of the way to the Corner in silence. The rest of that day moved slowly despite the constant flow of customers in and out of the shop's front door. The Corner felt sluggish and cold, and the afternoon rainstorm, drizzling tiredly, seemed to echo its mood.

As the days continued to pass hesitantly by, stores continued closing. Andy's fears continued to come to fruition as food providers in Capital Springs failed in their attempts to keep up with the required inadequate grocery prices. By forcibly establishing Nourishaid reimbursement rates as the standard price for everything provided by grocery stores, Mayor Stride Pen and the city government were rapidly making it more difficult for grocers to remain in business. The worst consequence of all was that as more stores closed their doors, the city's people had fewer places to go to receive the food they needed.

Eventually, the only grocery stores still in operation were Good Grocers, a large chain of stores, and a very small number of neighborhood grocers, among which was Johnston's Corner Market. It was now the only grocery store still selling food within an eight-block radius.

Supply and Demand

"It's getting cold out there!" Karl exclaimed one morning as he entered the Corner, stamping the wetness from his shoes. The winter day was chilly and damp, soaking through the shoes, gloves, and coats of those who ventured out. "How's it going, Andy?"

Ignoring the question, Andy contented himself with saying, "Hi, Karl. How are things?"

"Things are all right. Are you hanging in there?" Karl persisted, frowning. "Things have seemed a little bit off the past few times I've been in here."

"Still just trying to get by…somehow," answered Andy. He realized that his answer was vague and decided he owed his friend more.

"You're right, though, things are a little bit off around here," Andy explained. "I mean, you can see it, I can see it, we're all seeing it, but nothing's being done—nothing's being fixed. These new prices that Pen's making us follow are literally running every grocery store out of business. It's only a matter of time before they're all gone! I don't even know how the Corner's made it this far, but we're barely hanging on."

"Yeah, I've definitely been seeing and hearing about all the store closures," Karl said, leaning an elbow on the counter. Suddenly, his expression brightened. "But doesn't that also mean that there will be more people who have to come here to shop? Which might help you guys stay open in the long run, right?" he asked, hoping for his friend's sake that he sounded optimistic.

"Not really," Andy answered, shaking his head. "The only thing the Food Cost Balancing Act has accomplished is to create a massive demand on a very limited supply of food. There is no way that Stephen and I, along with the few other stores still in business, can provide

111

enough food for the entire city—especially while operating with the type of losses we're forced into taking. The bottom line is that although food prices are lower, fewer people can actually get their food."

At this reminder, Andy's mind ran over the myriad problems he faced, as it had countless times before over the past few weeks. Now that the Corner had become one of the last remaining grocery stores in Capital Springs, Andy and Stephen were inundated with customers from all over the city. It was becoming a regular occurrence to completely run out of food. Shoppers complained of racing from store to store hoping to find food still available, but without success.

Similarly, because Andy and Stephen were not allowed to charge customers according to the actual costs of food, the Corner's selection of groceries was significantly reduced. No longer could they afford to offer a variety of baked goods, high-quality and organic produce, or exotic products. Their sole focus was limiting losses, and this meant stocking their shelves with only the cheapest, most common goods.

The Corner's front door swung open to admit a customer, causing Andy to jerk his attention back to the here and now. "While the government and Mayor Stride Pen keep bragging about how low food prices are, they never admit that it's because there are now only a limited number of people able to get the groceries they need from such a limited and overworked food supply," Andy concluded.

Karl gave a low whistle. "I could tell things were getting bad, but I guess I didn't realize just how bad it was," he replied. "Well, I don't know what to do. Maybe the only way out is for the government to fix it all—they started the mess; they ought to clean it up. It is hard, though, to trust the guys who started all the problems in the first place."

"Well, all I know is that my hands are pretty much tied. There's not a lot I can do right now. We'll just keep going and see what happens in the future," Andy said.

From Grocer to Government Employee

Shortly after Andy's conversation with Karl, Mayor Stride Pen did indeed address the latest series of food problems facing the city. He announced that in an effort to curtail the problem of widespread store closures and to ensure that food provision reached adequate levels, all food distribution within Capital Springs would become a "public service," fully operated and administered by the city government.

The mayor insisted that, once again, the city was suffering as a result of greedy grocers, who were still unwilling to simply provide food in an accessible way. Continuing to rely on the typical empty complaints against food providers, he argued that owners of the city's remaining grocery stores were taking advantage of the larger customer base left to them by the closures of other stores, and that they were now trying to squeeze the largest possible profits out of desperate customers.

Under Mayor Stride Pen's new "public service" model of food distribution, the government would now pay for and provide all food used in the city. On top of this, all grocery stores would now be completely controlled by the city government, thus making grocers themselves government employees.

With food distribution and provision fully in the hands of the city government, we will finally achieve completely affordable food prices and totally accessible groceries, the voice of Mayor Stride Pen sounded through the radio's speakers and into the Corner. *We have made wonderful progress as a city and a community, and, now, every person in Capital Springs will be able to obtain whatever food they may need whenever they may need it. This great city will at last provide for its people.*

"He needs to visit a grocery store if he thinks that's going on anywhere in this city," Stephen burst out, interrupting the broadcast. "That guy's got to be crazy to say what he's saying. We've got hardly anything on our shelves, none of the food is as good as it used to be, and we've got lines out the door every day! We can't sell our food for what we should be, so we can't supply enough food to sell to everybody, and, in the end, fewer people are leaving here with food for themselves—so these lower prices he keeps talking about don't even matter!"

"Unfortunately, you're right," Andy replied sadly. "I wish he'd come visit us sometime too, and see what things are really like instead of constantly bragging and telling lies, trying to make us believe what he says rather than what we see going on in the real world."

Andy looked at the visibly dispirited customers currently in the store and continued. "In retrospect, I wonder if anyone making these policies ever really thought that they would work. Could anyone really have thought that these policies over the past several years would result in more food to more people at less expensive prices? Or did they know all along that this would never work, and one day they would have to use the so-called 'greed' of grocers as an excuse to simply have the government take over the entire system? Was this the plan all along?"

Shopping Segregation

Despite the mayor's frequent speeches of praise for the Food Cost Balancing Act and the city's new "public service" model, the people of Capital Springs were becoming increasingly frustrated and frantic. The voices of dissent and warning that had questioned Mayor Stride Pen during his earlier food reform campaigns were once again making themselves heard after being temporarily buried beneath the weight of the mayor's laws and policies. The citizens of Capital Springs cried out to the mayor's office, speaking of long lines, empty shelves and pantries, less food, and more hunger. The lower prices, the people began yelling, were no longer important if it meant that no food was available!

Despite the brewing mutiny, though, Mayor Stride Pen refused to change his stance or alter his thinking. He persistently delivered speeches lauding his reforms as progressive and essential while ignoring the dilemmas being faced by the city's people on a daily basis.

Eventually, though, the proverbial camel's back was broken. As it became clear that the government was unwilling to loosen its stranglehold on the city's food distribution system, people began acting on their own. Small shops that were owned and operated entirely independently of the city government sprung up. Because the city had taken complete control of all previously existing grocery stores, these new stores were able to operate beyond the control of the city's "public service" scheme, and, as a result, were able to supply a wide variety of food for anybody willing to pay for groceries using their own funds.

These new private stores immediately began operating in the same ways that grocery stores had prior to the introduction of Nourishaid and its subsequent layers of laws, codes, regulations, and restrictions. In comparison to the stores trapped in the mayor's "public service" food system, the owners of these stores stocked their shelves with a wider selection of food and products. They sold whatever their customers wanted, but the efforts to sell and provide food completely free of the city government naturally meant that prices for their groceries were more expensive than those in the city's "public service" stores.

The new privately operated stores met with instant popularity since food was now available once again at prices that had been considered reasonable before the coming of Nourishaid. Naturally, there was a waiting market. People enjoyed the ability to once again have access to many different types and qualities of food. If an individual wanted to spend the money for fancy imported cheese, he or she could again enjoy a wheel of Brie or a wedge of Roquefort. If someone wanted a steak of organic, grass-fed beef, he or she could pay the higher prices and have a mouth-watering filet.

Not surprisingly, Andy and Stephen quickly noticed the change these stores were making on the city's food distribution system. All customers who were willing and able to pay for their own food began leaving the Corner and shopping at the smaller, newer, private stores.

"Isn't this ironic?" Andy asked Stephen one evening while preparing to close the Corner for the evening. It had been another busy day with lines spilling through the door and onto the cold sidewalk outside as people waited for their turn to shop for groceries. As was now common, by mid-afternoon Andy and Stephen had completely run out of some of the more popular and common food products, and as a result had to watch many of those who had waited in line for so long leave with nothing.

"In the government's attempts to create some system that would guarantee food for every single person in the city, they've made things worse and more segregated than it ever has been," Andy mused. "Now the bottom line is money, because the size of your bank account determines where you shop. You can tell who's a 'have' and who's a 'have-not' by where he gets his groceries…and all because someone thought it would be a good idea to make everything available to everyone… assuming that was really their intent from the beginning."

"You're totally right," agreed Stephen. "The whole thing has been completely crazy. By forcing all grocery stores to sell their food for the exact same prices—prices too low to even make enough money to stay in business—everyone started closing their doors."

He paused to pick up a crumpled shopping list from the floor, then continued.

"The government thought they were making food more available to people, but they actually made it harder to get since the few shops that somehow survived the whole ordeal can't keep up with the overwhelming demands of feeding the entire city. And now that these private stores have started popping up, things are completely divided. Anyone with money goes to the small private shops and has access to any food they would ever need, while anyone without enough money has to still wait here in line for the government stores, just to discover that all the food's already run out."

"I'd say you pretty well summed it up," said Andy with a slight smile. Despite the trials and struggles he and Stephen had gone through together in working at the Corner, he was proud of the way his son had grown. He had become smarter and more aware. He understood what was going on around him and was able to comprehend the real-world effects of ideas and theories.

"The only thing the government's done in its quest to provide food for everyone is to create a new two-tiered system," Andy concluded. "People with money have access to food. People without money don't."

A Lesson in Economics

The inequalities in access to food among the city's population soon became apparent to many, causing a great deal of tension throughout Capital Springs. Sensing the growing strife in his city, it didn't take long for Mayor Stride Pen to address the issue. Again failing to understand that this latest problem was yet another symptom of his harmful food distribution policies, he quickly pushed a new law through to the city council for a vote.

It is not uncommon for disruptive forces to interfere with progress at the very moment when victory is within reach, and this is exactly what has occurred in our city. Just as the city government gained control of the entire food distribution system of Capital Springs, thereby guaranteeing that all people have access to food, greedy individuals have thwarted our progress.

It was the day before Mayor Stride Pen's new law would be voted upon, and his speech was being broadcast throughout the city.

Selfish individuals have defied the government and opened small, elite grocery stores beyond the control of the government. These stores work to create contention and dissension among us by offering food at exorbitant prices—prices too high for the working man or woman to ever afford. By attempting to make profits, owners of these stores have effectively discriminated against anyone not among the city's financial elite.

Naturally, those wealthy individuals who support such establishments by buying groceries from them are also to blame for the current economic gap. By leaving the city's public service grocery stores for private ones, they not only begin to deteriorate our progressive system of food distribution, but they also create unnecessary differences among our people. They attempt to separate themselves and create a small class of economic elites. For these reasons, I hope that the city council will tomorrow vote in favor of outlawing these harmful private grocery stores. A favorable vote tomorrow will allow our city to once again work toward providing food and equality for all.

Not surprisingly, the city council voted the mayor's proposal into law, and, as a result, all forms of privately owned and operated grocery stores were permanently closed. Furthermore, it became illegal to again open such stores. With all other options officially and thoroughly eliminated, every person in Capital Springs was once again forced to obtain food through the city government's "public service" food providers.

Stores became more crowded, lines were longer, food quality dropped, and overall access to food decreased. The residents of Capital Springs became angry. The city's newspapers, televisions, and radio stations were filled with people speaking out against the city government and its ineffective form of food provision.

"It's all basic economics," Andy began explaining to Stephen. The hour was early, and the Corner had yet to open for the day. Andy had just finished reading a letter to the editor of *The City* in which complaints regarding the difficulty of obtaining groceries were voiced. "I mean, really basic. Stuff I've learned and figured out just by selling groceries all my life. The basic problem here is that anytime price caps are put onto anything, there's going to be a shortage of that very thing."

Stephen walked over and sat down on the stool behind the front counter to listen to his father speak.

"Like I said, it's all economics. Supply and demand. Incentives, choices, and decisions," Andy continued, settling into his role as instructor. "So, let's imagine that rent in a certain neighborhood is capped at some low price that everyone can afford with no problem. Well, it might seem good without really thinking it through, because obviously the rent is cheaper and more affordable."

Stephen nodded. "That makes sense, I guess."

Andy held up a finger. "But see, what *really* ends up happening is that there gradually become fewer and fewer apartments available to rent out because real estate investors and builders—any potential landlords—have no incentive to build or make available new apartment buildings. With the price caps, they just won't earn enough money to make all the effort and overhead costs worth it. So, in order to get an apartment at all, you have to become friends with a government bureaucrat in charge of housing."

"I definitely see that happening with us right now," Stephen said, an intense look on his face as he thought the issue through for himself. "That's the same reason that so many stores went out of business, but no new ones are opening up. Grocers couldn't make any money with those really low prices we were forced into by the government. It's a struggle just to keep the doors open—forget about actually making any type of good income."

"That's for sure," Andy agreed, looking pointedly at the cash register.

"So," Stephen continued, "after stores start closing down because they're unable to handle the losses forced on them by the price caps, there's no one else crazy enough to get into the business, knowing that they'll probably just be losing money the whole time."

"Exactly," Andy nodded. "The other thing that happens is that because there are so many people who need the service, whether it's apartments, food, or whatever, the people selling or renting the product have no reason to put effort into keeping their product really high quality. A landlord who's forced to rent her apartment for a low price has no reason to renovate it. There are so many people willing to rent *any* apartment since there's a limited number of them out there that landlords will end up offering old, dumpy apartments for the artificially low rent prices."

This time, it was Stephen who cast a meaningful glance at the shelves bearing generic and low-cost goods.

"Wow, that's happening with us too!" he exclaimed, interested in how closely the ideas his father was describing were actually coming true all around him. "The few grocery stores still selling food have been pretty much forced into selling cheap stuff. We've had to do that too. We obviously can't afford to sell high-quality, more expensive, fresh food for the super-low prices imposed on us by the government, but what you're saying is that we also have no reason to go through all the effort to stock up on really nice, new stuff because everyone's going to buy what we have either way."

"Yeah, exactly. Like I said, this is all just simple and basic economics," Andy repeated. "By putting price caps on all the food in the city, Mayor Stride Pen has done two really harmful things." He held up one finger. "First, he's removed any incentive for anybody to provide food at all, which means that although grocery prices are lower, there's less food available to the people, which is why we all have lines going clear out to the street."

Andy paused and held up a second finger. "Second, he's made it impossible to sell any high-quality or unique food, not only because we simply can't afford to provide more expensive groceries, but also because he's created a huge group of people who are willing to buy anything—at this point, people are just excited to have food at all."

"Mmm-hmmm." Stephen looked out the window where, as if to prove his father's point, several dejected-looking people were already waiting for the Corner to open.

"The bottom line," Andy concluded, "is that these are all simple laws of economics that have always been around, and we, as a city, have broken them."

Too Little, Too Late

With the entire population of Capital Springs thrust back onto the government's public food distribution system, food providers frantically attempted to keep up with the heavy demand and the fast pace. Customers were equally frantic, rushing to claim a spot in line well before stores opened in the morning with the hope of making it inside while food would still be available and on the shelves.

The entire situation became unbearably frustrating to all involved, and many individuals and families began leaving the city to do their grocery shopping. Despite the long distances they were required to travel to neighboring cities, many of those able to afford the trip thought it well worth the inconvenience to buy whatever groceries they needed and wanted.

Meanwhile, the food provision system of Capital Springs only grew worse. Already at a dangerously low level, the number of operating grocery stores in the city continued to decrease. Every so often, another store collapsed and closed its doors. And when that happened, no one stepped in to fill the vacancy. Understandably, nobody wanted to enter a field in which there was no freedom to run a business the way one saw fit, and in which the entire focus was on simply avoiding bankruptcy. The limitations and extreme restrictions the city government had placed on grocers had become so overwhelming that they were driving away all future generations of food providers.

Andy and Stephen managed to help Johnston's Corner Market crawl through the winter, and by the time hints of spring were felt in the air, the Corner was the last grocery store still in operation for an entire fifteen-block radius. Every day was now a maniacal sprint to open the doors, handle a flood of frenzied customers, and somehow keep inventory up in order to meet the demand. They were now selling the cheapest food they could find. Nothing was fresh or interesting. It was all packaged in the same white plastic, and it all had the same stale taste, but it was all the Corner could afford to sell.

After Mayor Stride Pen commandeered the city's entire food distribution system, these were the final results. The most devastating outcome of the city government's food distribution policies, however, was the fact that the number of people with access to food had now fallen lower than it ever had been. In the government's attempts to ensure food for all people, the only thing created was a faulty system in which only a comparatively few people were able to eat very undesirable food.

The frenzy continued to build. Windows of stores were occasionally smashed during the night, and shelves were looted by hungry people sick of waiting in lines only to be turned away by empty aisles and shelves. People now did whatever they could to obtain food. Complaints against the city government continued. Protests in front of City Hall became common. The people of the city now knew exactly what their problems were and where they came from, and they demanded that the government back away from the process of food provision.

It was clear to most people that politicians on all sides had repeatedly refused to change their thinking, their campaigning, their lobbying for votes, and that finally, things were about to collapse. The citizens of Capital Springs, it seemed, had finally figured out the dilemmas facing food distribution, but their realizations were too late. In a twist of dark irony, the very people now raising the voice of dissent were the same ones who earlier had voted politicians like Mayor Ted Sprine and Mayor Stride Pen into office. This was the city that had asked for and praised the various food distribution laws that had led to the current predicament.

All the changes, restrictions, and laws now surrounding food were voted for and enacted without considering what it all really meant. Now that the final outcomes had become painfully apparent, people wanted an escape, but the heavy metal door forged in the fires of political machinations and hardened under the pressure of incomplete thought had already clanged shut.

The city hovered on the brink of total chaos, and Andy knew it.

The End

Walking to work one morning through the early dampness of March, Andy and Stephen saw a crowd of people—a quick, uneven body of irritated motion—in front of the Corner. They immediately knew this was not the forming of the usual early morning lines, for as they drew nearer, people began yelling and sprinting away in all directions.

The crowd dispersed, frantically spilling across the sidewalk and road. People ran as quickly as they could with arms full of boxes and tin cans, glancing fearfully at Andy and Stephen over their shoulders as they fled.

"Hey!" Andy yelled as he and Stephen pursued the looters. "What do you think you're doing? Damn it!"

His protests were in vain. The crowd of people had disappeared into the gloom of dark windows and dirty brick buildings. Andy and Stephen were left alone, standing quietly before the smashed remains of the store's front window.

Shards of glass covered the linoleum floor of Johnston's Corner Market as Andy and Stephen stepped through the window's gaping wound. The shelves were empty. Many lay mangled on the ground, toppled in the frenzy of the desperate looters.

Andy bent down and picked up a smashed soda can, its contents still leaking out onto the floor. After examining it closely, he dropped it onto the ground. "We can't do this anymore," he said softly to Stephen. They stood at the front counter looking out over the demolished ruins of their beloved grocery store. "We've finally been run out of business. There's nothing left for us here. We've done our very best, and we've done all we could possibly do."

Shaking his head, he repeated, "We can't do this anymore."

Together, Andy and Stephen stepped past the upturned shelves, back through the broken window, and slowly walked away down the damp, cold sidewalk.

United States Healthcare Timeline

PRE-1900

People are typically treated in their homes, paying physicians out of pocket, while hospitals are usually reserved for the medically indigent. Such hospitals are financed through taxes and charity organizations.

<u>1798:</u> Congress establishes the National Marine Health Service, originally financed by 20-cent deductions from seamen's wages. This service is later renamed the Public Health Service.

Rapid urbanization brought about by the Industrial Revolution gives rise to voluntary hospitals, where patients pay for treatment.

1900-1910

<u>1908:</u> Worker's compensation laws are passed for federal employees.

1910-1920

<u>1917</u>: Public Health Service facilities are authorized to provide medical care to World War I veterans with service-connected disabilities.

<u>1918</u>: The Chamberlain-Kahn Act authorizes the first federal grants to states for public health services.

1920-1930

<u>1921</u>: The Sheppard-Towner Act is passed, authorizing federal aid to states for maternity, child healthcare, and welfare programs. In 1922, this act is ruled unconstitutional by the Supreme Court.

1930-1940

<u>1933</u>: The Federal Emergency Relief Administration provides some medical, dental, and nursing services for indigent populations.

<u>1935</u>: On August 14, the Social Security Act is passed, originally omitting health insurance.

<u>1937</u>: The Railroad Retirement Act is passed, providing services to survivors and dependents of railroad workers.

1940-1950

<u>1943</u>: Emergency Maternity and Infancy Care is authorized, seeming "to some to be a precedent that could ease the passage at war's end of a health insurance system for the general public" (Corning).

<u>1943</u>: The Wagner-Murray-Dingell bill is introduced, calling for various additions to Social Security, including measures for health insurance; the bill does not pass.

1945: President Truman sends a revised version of the Wagner-Murray-Dingell bill to Congress, which again fails to pass.

During WWII, in the face of wartime wage and price controls, employers begin offering and providing healthcare coverage as incentives to employees.

1950-1960

1950: The federal government "enacts [a] program of direct payments to 'medical vendors' for the treatment of welfare clients, including the elderly" (Corning).

1956: Congress passes the Dependents Medical Care Act, which extends government-funded health services to military dependents and allows for the receipt of treatment from private healthcare providers. This, along with the Military Medical Benefits Amendments of 1966, led to the creation of the Civilian Health and Medical Program of the Uniformed Services, now known as TRICARE.

1960-1970

1960: The Kerr-Mills bill is signed into law, expanding "the program of medical vendor payments provided under the State-run public assistance programs" by "creating a new assistance category called 'medical indigency' for elderly people who might not otherwise qualify for welfare in their States but who needed help with their medical bills"(Corning).

1962: Migrant Health Act provides federal funding directed at providing health services for migrant populations.

1965: Social Security amendments authorize Medicare and Medicaid programs.

<u>1967</u>: The Early Periodic Screening, Diagnosis, and Treatment Program is created to provide screening and health services for children under Medicaid.

1970-1980

<u>1971</u>: President Richard Nixon's Economic Stabilization Program enacts price controls on various hospital costs; these controls end in 1974.

<u>1972</u>: Social Security amendments include numerous acts aimed at both cost containment and expansion of Medicare eligibility.

<u>1977</u>: Aimed at improving the general administration of both Medicare and Medicaid, both programs are brought together under the Health Care Financing Administration.

<u>1978</u>: Under Section 222 of the 1972 Social Security Amendments, New Jersey experiments with alternative healthcare provider reimbursement schemes, eventually opting for a prospective payment plan. This then becomes a model for the federal government's exploration of such a system (see Mayes).

1980-1990

<u>1981</u>: The Omnibus Budget Reconciliation Act calls for significant reductions in funding for many federal health programs.

<u>1982</u>: Under President Ronald Reagan, the Tax Equity and Fiscal Responsibility Act initiates further reductions in several federal health programs, many of which help set the stage for the final transition to the Prospective Payment System (see Mayes).

<u>1983</u>: Social Security amendments call for the change to the Medicare Prospective Payment System (PPS), in which payments are based on Diagnosis-Related Groups (DRGs).

<u>1984:</u> The Deficit Reduction Act includes amendments designed to limit Medicare and Medicaid expenditures.

<u>1984:</u> The Child Health Assistance Program requires states to expand their Medicaid programs to include more low-income pregnant women and children.

<u>1985:</u> The Emergency Medical Treatment and Active Labor Act passes, introducing new requirements for hospital emergency room treatments and procedures.

<u>1986:</u> The Consolidated Omnibus Budget Reconciliation Act and the Sixth Omnibus Budget Reconciliation Act introduce various changes to the Medicare and Medicaid programs.

<u>1987:</u> The Omnibus Budget Reconciliation Act schedules significant reductions in Medicare spending, a large portion of which are accomplished by limiting increases in healthcare provider reimbursement rates (which occur to account for such factors as inflation); this act also expands eligibility for groups of pregnant women and children.

<u>1989:</u> The Omnibus Budget Reconciliation Act includes $2.7 billion in Medicare reductions, the majority of which come through delays or restrictions in PPS payment increases.

1990-2000

<u>1990:</u> The Budget Reconciliation Act of 1990 includes Medicare reforms intended to save $40 billion in federal expenditures over five years.

<u>1990:</u> The Health Care Financing Administration enacts a 1.22 percent reduction of all DRG weights.

<u>1996:</u> The Health Insurance Portability and Accountability Act passes, introducing, among other things, a series of new rules, regulations, and requirements for healthcare providers.

<u>1999:</u> The Ticket to Work and Work Incentives Improvement Act expands Medicare and Medicaid eligibility.

2000-2010

<u>2003:</u> The Medicare Modernization Act is signed into law by President George W. Bush, initiating a series of major changes to Medicare, which includes a new drug benefit.

<u>2010:</u> On March 21, Congress gives final approval for President Barack Obama's sweeping healthcare reform, which is designed to overhaul much of the nation's healthcare system with special attention paid to significantly cutting healthcare costs and expanding coverage to millions of uninsured Americans.

Works Cited

Corning, Peter A. "The Evolution of Medicare…From Idea to Law." 1969. *Social Security Online.* July 2009 <http://www.socialsecurity.gov/history/corning.html>.

Dafny, Leemore S. "How Do Hospitals Respond to Price Changes?" *American Economic Review* 95.5 (December 2005): 1525-1547.

"Health Care Reform Timeline." 2011. *Timelines.* April 2010 <http://timelines.com/topics/health-care-reform>.

John Q. Dir. Nick Cassevetes. Perf. Denzel Washington and Anne Heche. New Line Cinema, 2002.

Mayes, Rick. "The Origins, Development, and Passage of Medicare's Revolutionary Prospective Payment System." *Journal of the History of Medicine and Allied Sciences* 62.1 (2006): 21-55.

Reid, T.R. *The Healing of America: A Global Quest for Better, Cheaper, and Fairer Health Care.* New York: Penguin Books, 2009.

"Key Milestones in CMS Programs." 2010. *Centers for Medicare and Medicaid Services.* July 2009 <https://www.cms.gov/History/Downloads/CMSProgramKeyMilestones.pdf>.

"World Health Organization Assesses the World's Health Systems." 21 June 2000. *World Health Organization.* August 2009 <http://www.who.int/inf-pr-2000/en/pr2000-44.html>.

Resources

Accelerate the momentum of your Healthcare Flywheel®.

Access additional resources at
www.firestarterpublishing.com/overourheads.

ABOUT STUDER GROUP:

Studer Group® works with over 800 healthcare organizations in the U.S. and beyond, teaching them how to achieve, sustain, and accelerate exceptional clinical, operational, and financial outcomes.

As the metrics our industry publically reports get expanded—and as reimbursement is increasingly tied to these results—organizations are forced to get progressively better at providing top quality care with fewer dollars. We help our partners install an execution framework called Evidence-Based Leadership℠ (EBL) that aligns their goals, actions, and processes. This framework creates the foundation that enables them to transform the way they provide care in this era of rapid change.

EBL creates a culture of execution that empowers organizations to respond to new initiatives more quickly and effectively than the rest of the nation. In fact, the EBL framework we coach our partners to implement helps them accelerate the rate of improvement and efficiency in their clinical care and also maximizes reimbursement. EBL also leads to favorable HCAHPS results and core measures and reduces the occurrence of hospital-acquired conditions and preventable readmissions.

We practice what we teach. Within our own organization, Studer Group uses the same evidence-based approaches to accelerate and sustain high performance through better employee engagement and customer loyalty. As a result, we received the Malcolm Baldrige National Quality Award in 2010—and have consistently been recognized as one of the best small companies to work for in America.

BOOKS: categorized by audience

Senior Leaders & Physicians
Leadership and Medicine—A book that makes sense of the complex challenges of healthcare and offers a wealth of practical advice to future generations, written by Floyd D. Loop, MD, former chief executive of the Cleveland Clinic (1989-2004).

Engaging Physicians: A Manual to Physician Partnership—A tactical and passionate roadmap for physician collaboration to generate organizational high performance, written by Stephen C. Beeson, MD.

Straight A Leadership: Alignment, Action, Accountability—A guide that will help you identify gaps in Alignment, Action, and Accountability, create a plan to fill them, and become a more resourceful, agile, high-performing organization, written by Quint Studer.

Physicians
Excellence with an Edge: Practicing Medicine in a Competitive Environment—An insightful book that provides practical tools and

techniques you need to know to have a solid grasp of the business side of making a living in healthcare, written by Michael T. Harris, MD.

Practicing Excellence: A Physician's Manual to Exceptional Health Care—This book, written by Stephen C. Beeson, MD, is a brilliant guide to implementing physician leadership and behaviors that will create a high-performance workplace.

All Leaders

The HCAHPS Handbook: Hardwire Your Hospital for Pay-for-Performance Success—Three Studer Group experts—Quint Studer, Brian Robinson, and Karen Cook, RN—explore the significance of HCAHPS to our industry's future and offer specific tactics aimed at helping hospitals achieve and sustain improved results on each survey composite.

Hardwiring Excellence—A *Business Week* bestseller, this book is a road map to creating and sustaining a "Culture of Service and Operational Excellence" that drives bottom-line results.
Written by Quint Studer

Results That Last—A Wall Street Journal bestseller by Quint Studer that teaches leaders in every industry how to apply his tactics and strategies to their own organizations to build a corporate culture that consistently reaches and exceeds its goals.

Hardwiring Flow: Systems and Processes for Seamless Patient Care—Drs. Thom Mayer and Kirk Jensen delve into one of the most critical issues facing healthcare leaders today: patient flow.

Eat That Cookie!: Make Workplace Positivity Pay Off...For Individuals, Teams, and Organizations—Written by Liz Jazwiec, RN, this book is funny, inspiring, relatable, and is packed with realistic, down-to-earth tactics to infuse positivity into your culture.

"I'm Sorry to Hear That..." Real Life Responses to Patients' 101 Most Common Complaints About Health Care—When you respond to a patient's complaint, you are responding to the patient's sense of help-lessness and anxiety. The service recovery scripts offered in this book can help you recover a patient's confidence in you and your organization. Authored by Susan Keane Baker and Leslie Bank.

What's Right in Health Care: 365 Stories of Purpose, Worthwhile Work, and Making a Difference—A collaborative effort of stories from healthcare professionals across the nation. This 742-page book shares a story a day submitted by your friends and colleagues. It is a daily reminder about why we answered this calling and why we stay with it—to serve a purpose, to do worthwhile work, and to make a difference.

101 Answers to Questions Leaders Ask—By Quint Studer and Studer Group coaches, offers practical, prescriptive solutions to some of the many questions he's received from healthcare leaders around the country.

Nurse Leaders and Nurses
The Nurse Leader Handbook: The Art and Science of Nurse Leadership—By Studer Group senior nursing and physician leaders from across the country, is filled with knowledge that provides nurse leaders with a solid foundation for success. It also serves as a reference they can revisit again and again when they have questions or need a quick refresher course in a particular area of the job.

Inspired Nurse and Inspired Journal—By Rich Bluni, RN, helps maintain and recapture the inspiration nurses felt at the start of their journey with action-oriented "spiritual stretches" and stories that il-luminate those sacred moments we all experience.

Emergency Department Team
Excellence in the Emergency Department—A book by Stephanie Baker, RN, CEN, MBA, is filled with proven, easy-to-implement, step-by-step instructions that will help you move your Emergency Department forward.

For more information about books and other resources, visit www.firestarterpublishing.com.

SOFTWARE SOLUTIONS:

Leader Evaluation Manager™: Results Through Focus and Accountability
Studer Group's Leader Evaluation Manager is a web-based application that automates the goal setting and performance review process for all leaders, while ensuring that the performance metrics of individual leaders are aligned with the overall goals of the organization. By using Leader Evaluation Manager, both leaders and their supervisors will clearly understand from the beginning of the year what goals need to be accomplished to achieve a successful annual review, can plan quarterly tasks with completion targets under each goal, and view monthly report cards to manage progress.

To learn more, please visit www.firestarterpublishing.com.

INSTITUTES:

Taking You and Your Organization to the Next Level with Quint Studer
Learn the tools, tactics, and strategies that are needed to Take You and Your Organization to the Next Level at this two-day institute with Quint Studer and Studer Group's Coach Experts. You will walk away

with your passion ignited, and with Evidence-Based Leadership^{SM} strategies to create a sustainable culture of excellence.

Nuts and Bolts of Operational Excellence in the Emergency Department

Improve patient flow and build service and operational excellence in your Emergency Department as Jay Kaplan, MD, FACEP, and Stephanie Baker, RN, CEN, MBA, both with extensive and ongoing real-life ED experience, share proven tactics such as Provider in Triage, Rounding for Outcomes, Discharge Phone Calls, Key Words at Key Times, and AIDET^{SM}.

What's Right in Health Care^{SM}

One of the largest healthcare peer-to-peer learning conferences in the nation, *What's Right in Health Care* brings organizations together to share ideas that have been proven to make healthcare better.

To review a listing of Studer Group institutes or to register for an institute, visit www.studergroup.com/institutes.

For information on Continuing Education Credits, visit www.studergroup.com/cmecredits.

Visit www.firestarterpublishing.com/overourheads to access and download many of the resources, examples, and tools mentioned in *Over Our Heads*.

About the Author

Rulon F. Stacey, PhD, FACHE, was recognized as having achieved a major milestone when, in November 2008, the president of the United States announced that the Poudre Valley Health System (PVHS), an organization led by Dr. Stacey for more than a decade, had been selected to receive the prestigious Malcolm Baldrige National Quality Award, the nation's highest honor in performance excellence. In 2010, the American College of Healthcare Executives Council of Regents selected Dr. Stacey as ACHE chair-elect, and he will assume responsibilities as board chair of the governing board of ACHE in March 2011.

Dr. Stacey has spent the entirety of his adult life working in the healthcare industry and has actively addressed various healthcare issues. His career began while serving on active duty in the United States Air Force, where he was recognized for his achievements in the Medical Service Corps. Following his time in the military, Dr. Stacey worked as

CEO of St. Vincent General Hospital in Leadville, Colorado, before becoming chief operating officer of the 400-bed St. Francis Hospital and Health Center in Chicago. In 1996, he became CEO of PVHS.

Beginning his time at PVHS, Dr. Stacey was the organization's fifth CEO in four years. He has since transformed the organization into an important leader in the healthcare industry, winning various local and national quality distinctions, including recognition as the only two-time winner of the Colorado Performance Excellence Institute's PEAK Award, and culminating with the Malcolm Baldrige National Quality Award.

In 1999, ACHE recognized Dr. Stacey as Young Healthcare Executive of the Year. In 2004, he was elected by his peers as Colorado Regent of ACHE, and in 2007, as one of the twelve-member Board of Governors of ACHE.

As a result of his achievements, Dr. Stacey is a regular voice both nationally and internationally, speaking and lecturing on such subjects as performance excellence, leadership, and healthcare reform.

How to Order Additional Copies of

Over Our Heads:
An Analogy on Healthcare, Good Intentions and Unforeseen Consequences

Orders may be placed:

Online at:
www.firestarterpublishing.com
www.studergroup.com

By phone at: 866-354-3473

By mail at: Fire Starter Publishing
913 Gulf Breeze Parkway, Suite 6
Gulf Breeze, FL 32561

(Bulk discounts are available.)

Over Our Heads
is also available online at www.amazon.com.